Knowing the Score: Preserving Collections of Music

Compiled by Mark Roosa and Jane Gottlieb

MLA Technical Report No. 23

Music Library Association, Inc.
Canton, Mass.

Association for Library Collections & Technical Services
Chicago, Illinois
1994

The Music Library Association

P.O. Box 487, Canton, MA 02021

Copyright © 1994 by Music Library Association. All rights reserved. The paper in this publication meets the minimum requirements of American National Standard for Information Sciences—Permanence of Paper for Printed Library Materials, ANSI Z39.48-1984. ∞

ISSN: 0094-5099

ISBN: 0-914954-48-2

MLA Technical Reports
Series Editor
Richard P. Smiraglia

Library of Congress Cataloging in Publication Data

Knowing the score : preserving collections of music / compiled by Mark Roosa and Jane Gottlieb.
    p. cm. — (MLA technical report, ISSN 0094-5099 ; no. 23)
    Consists chiefly of papers presented at an Association for Library Collections & Technical Services program of the same name, held during the 1991 annual conference of the American Library Association in Atlanta, Ga.
    Includes bibliographical references and index.
    ISBN 0-914954-48-2
    1. Music—Conservation and restoration—Congresses. 2. Sound recordings—Conservation and restoration—Congresses. I. Roosa, Mark. II. Gottlieb, Jane, 1954– . III. Series: MLA technical reports ; no. 23.
ML111.K65 1994
025.8′4—dc20   94-14390
                                                        CIP
                                                        MN

Contents

Introduction	1
Preface *Jane Gottlieb*	1
Opening Remarks *Mark Roosa*	2
Music: Why is it Different? *Susan T. Sommer*	5
Working Against the Odds: Preservation Approaches in a Conservatory Library *Jane Gottlieb*	12
Program Components	14
Survey Reports	15
Grant Funds	15
Preservation Projects At Juilliard	17
Environmental Considerations	24
Binding In-House	26
Unusual Score Formats	27
Paper Condition	29
Maintenance Decision-Making	29
Notes and References	34
A Condition Survey Of The Circulating Score Collection Of The Juilliard School *Elizabeth Sadewhite*	35
Survey Results	39
Descriptive Variables	39
Call # (Classification)	39
Country Of Publication	39
Copyright Date	40
Accession/Cataloging Date	40
Number of Pages	40
Signatures	41

CONTENTS

Origin of Binding	41
Binding Construction	42
Year of Last Circulation	42
Condition Variables	42
Cover	42
Condition of Binding	42
Paper Yellowing	44
Torn Paper	44
Pencil Markings	44
Other Markings	45
Previous Repair	45
Some Conclusions	45
References	50
Mass Deacidification At The Northwestern University Music Library	51
Kenneth Calkins	
Background	51
Selection Issues: the Rationale for Treating the Music Collection	52
Bibliographic Control	53
The DEZ Treatment Process	54
Quality Assurance	55
Treatment Costs, Quantities, and Timetables	56
Conclusions	57
Notes and References	58
Preservation of Moving Images and Sound Recordings in the Music Library	59
Gerald Gibson	
Basic Actions	60
Materials	61
Controlling Degradation	62
Environment	69
Conclusion	72

CONTENTS

References	74
Appendix A: Selected Bibliography	75
Sound Recordings	75
Magnetic Media	77
Appendix B: Preservation Supplies For Sound Recordings	81
Appendix C: Audio Reformatting Fact Sheets	84
Index	90

Introduction

PREFACE

Jane Gottlieb

This publication contains papers presented at the Association for Library Collections & Technical Services program, "Knowing the Score: Preserving Collections of Music," held during the 1991 American Library Association annual conference in Atlanta, Georgia. The program was conceived by the Education Committee of the Preservation of Library Materials Section and was cosponsored by the Music Library Association, the Public Library Association, and the Rare Books and Manuscripts section of the Association of College & Research Libraries. The planning committee for this program was chaired by Mark Roosa, and included Ellen Cunningham, Martha Hanson, Cheryl Shackelton, and Michele Cloonan as members. John Shepard (Chair, Music Library Association Preservation Committee), and Cheryl Shackelton helped organize an

---

Jane Gottlieb is Head Librarian at the Juilliard School in New York City. Prior to assuming this position, Ms. Gottlieb was Librarian at the Mannes School of Music (NYC). Ms. Gottlieb participates in the activities of METRO and serves on several preservation committees within that organization. She has served on the board of directors of the Music Library Association and is currently Vice-President/President-Elect. Ms. Gottlieb has edited three volumes from an ongoing series entitled *The Musical Woman: An International Perspective.*

Mark Roosa is Chief Preservation Officer at the Huntington Library, San Marino, Calif. Prior to coming to the Huntington he was Preservation Officer at the University of Delaware Library. In 1987, he was an Andrew W. Mellon Preservation Administration Intern in the Preservation Office at the Library of Congress. Mr. Roosa is a member of the American Library Association and serves on various committees within that organization. In 1989 he was an International Federation of Library Associations and Institutions (IFLA)/Vosper Fellow and he developed educational materials on the care, handling, and storage of non-book library materials.

extensive exhibit of protective enclosures that was mounted in conjunction with the program. These papers were gathered for publication in the summer of 1993. At that time, a condition survey of the score collections at the Juilliard School (by Elizabeth Sadewhite) and a report on a major project for the mass-deacidification of scores at Northwestern University (by Kenneth Calkins) were added to this volume. The Music Library Association and the Association for Library Collections & Technical Services are pleased to publish jointly this set of papers.

OPENING REMARKS
Mark Roosa

A year or so ago when I was asked to help plan a program on music preservation I jumped at the chance. As a performing musician and one who studied music in college, the topic of preserving music is especially dear to me. In some ways music is how I got into library preservation.

During my junior year in college I took a semester off and moved to New Orleans to study the music of the New Orleans brass bands. Upon my arrival there I went directly to the jazz archives where I was to conduct my research. After a few minutes in conversation with the resident archivist, who was a seasoned authority on New Orleans music, I knew had my work cut out for me. In addition to extensive reading, he suggested I also meet some of the musicians, attend a brass-band funeral, and listen to interviews the archives had taped with several of the early brass band musicians. He was not so sure of the condition of the tapes, so typed transcripts of the interviews would be provided instead. So, I consulted the catalog, gave him a list of topics, and a number of folders and boxes were brought out.

The first folder I opened pertained to the great New Orleans clarinetist George Lewis and it contained the usual range of stuff: scraps of paper, photographs, and some correspondence. Upon closer inspection I found a transcribed interview that had been painstakingly typed onto thin, yellow, somewhat dog-eared tissue paper. Holding those flimsy pages in my hands it hit me that not only were the words and impressions of this one musician at risk of being lost but that the story of an important New Orleans social and cultural institution was also disappearing before my eyes.

The notion that music and society are somehow inextricably linked is not new. Wasn't it Confucius who said, "If you want to know if people are well-governed, and if its laws are good or bad, examine the music it practices?" John Russell Young, former Librarian of Congress, echoed this line of thinking in a speech to Congress many years later when he stated, "Nothing better indicates the higher qualities of a people than their music." Indeed, some would argue that music also indicates the lower qualities of a people, but I think most of us would agree that it is both high and low together that best represents a societies' accomplishments, its conditions, and its aspirations. If in some real sense music is a "barometer of society," then the music library is the place of record where the creative expression, history, and literature of that society is collected, protected, consulted, and enjoyed.

When we speak of music collections, what exactly do we mean? Perhaps more important, why are the preservation problems of music collections different from those affecting regular collections? Don't music libraries contain books, journals, and manuscripts just as do most other libraries? Yes, but they also contain scores and performance parts, photographs and memorabilia (musical instruments, statues, etc.) audio tapes and discs, videotapes, films in all formats, and of course compact discs and videodiscs, all of which pose their own particular problems for storage, handling, and use.

INTRODUCTION

The goal of today's program is to provide us all with a better understanding of the unique challenges that await us as we preserve music collections for our library users. To this end our distinguished speakers will share with us their thoughts and insights as we travel into the unique and extraordinary world of the music library.

Music: Why is it different?

Susan T. Sommer

ABSTRACT: What preservation problems are unique to music or are most frequently encountered in dealing with it in libraries? What are music librarians doing about these problems? We should distinguish between two kinds of music, music we hear and music we see. To combat decay and obsolescence, the most frequent tactic employed by librarians to preserve recorded sound has been to transfer the material to another medium. Many preservation concerns music librarians face are identical with those of other librarians: brittle books, acidic papers, destructive foreign substances, problematic bindings, climatic conditions, and so forth. There are some important differences between printed music and the printed word, which add to the preservation problems of the librarian concerned with a collection of music. The nature of music notation is inherently different from the written word. Two axiomatic requirements for music in performance—legibility at a distance and openability—give rise to an important corollary:. music, compared to books, comes in odd sizes. Our message is that we, the music librarians, are ready to participate in preservation; in turn we need recognition of our expertise and the special requirements needed to preserve the rich musical heritage on our library shelves.

Music: Why is it different? In setting the scene I would like to address two questions. First, what preservation problems are unique to music or are most frequently encountered in dealing with it in libraries? And second, what are music librarians doing about these problems?

In the first place we should distinguish between two kinds of music, music we hear and music we see. In the first instance we are dealing, in a library context, with recorded sound. Recorded sound is a medium with a potentially enormous public. Unlike notated music, which calls for years of study before a musician can read it fluently, anyone can listen to—and potentially enjoy—virtually

---

Susan T. Sommer is Chief Librarian of the Circulating Collections at The New York Public Library for the Performing Arts at Lincoln Center.

6 MUSIC: WHY IS IT DIFFERENT?

anything that has been captured in this medium. The immediate accessibility of sound has increased the audience for music and the demand for both the music itself and information about it to an astonishing degree. Public libraries often have extensive circulating collections of recordings, frequently administered in tandem with videotapes, a medium with which they share many problems. Academic libraries also need sound recordings to support curricular needs in music and other departments.

But sound recordings also have important archival functions. Some forms of music are preserved *only* in recorded form either because there is no notated record of them or because existing notation is inadequate. Non-Western music, computer music, popular music composed in a studio and improvisational jazz are all examples of this. For Western art music, which has a highly developed notational system, recorded sound serves as the history of performance, preserving the performances of great artists of the past and documenting changing taste and aesthetic experiences.

Recorded sound is immediately distinguishable from most other materials in libraries. It doesn't look like a book; it's not on paper. You need additional equipment to access it. All of these set it apart and pose special problems of housing, conservation, and use. Recorded sound comes in a variety of shapes and sizes: flat discs, tiny cassettes, large reels, cylinders, all of which require different kinds of containers and shelving. Sound can be preserved on wax, acetate, on vinyl, on metal, on polymer tape, to name but a few media, each of which has a different chemical makeup and poses a different set of problems to the conservator. These scientific problems have by no means been solved. At this point, in fact, it would appear that all of these information-bearing substances are inherently unstable, some to an alarming degree.

Finally recorded sounds and images require different kinds of equipment to make their holdings comprehensible to human beings. A piece of tape or a cylinder will only reveal its contents when played through an appropriate piece of machinery, technology that varies with the format and medium employed. Capital expense, maintenance, and obsolescence are ongoing concerns in any library of recorded materials.

To combat decay and obsolescence, the most frequent tactic employed by librarians to preserve recorded sound has been to transfer the material to another medium. But we must recall that any reproduction or reformatting necessarily involves some loss of information. And there is no guarantee that the transfers will not themselves be subject to further processes of decay.

Any decision to pursue a conservation program actively involves spending money and setting priorities. As you will hear later, the task of preserving the music we hear is a particularly complex one. But with the rapid growth of non-print, non-paper holdings in other parts of the library—in CD-ROMs and video for example—libraries and preservation people should be looking increasingly toward music librarians and sound archivists for their expertise and experience in this field.

Turning to the problems of preserving notated music, it would appear that we are now on familiar ground. The music we see is customarily printed on paper and, at least in the case of substantial scores or collections, even *looks* like a book. Library conservators have decades of experience in dealing with books and paper; if the solutions are not easy, at least the problems have been identified.

Indeed many preservation concerns music librarians face are identical with those of other librarians: brittle books, acidic papers, destructive foreign substances, problematic bindings, climatic conditions, and so forth. Music librarians look to learn from our colleagues in conservation at every turn. Nevertheless there are some important differences between printed music and the printed word that add to the preservation problems of the librarian concerned with a collection of music.

8 MUSIC: WHY IS IT DIFFERENT?

The nature of music notation is inherently different from the written word. Most music in the Western world is represented in a graphic system employing special symbols to indicate the pitch and duration of various sounds appearing sequentially and/or simultaneously. Other indicators may also be present, for example, directions concerning speed, dynamics, phrasing, the text for vocal works, etc.

Pitch, the highness or lowness of various tones, is indicated on a grid called a staff on which are placed symbols for notes. The precise vertical placement of the notes and their alignment are a crucial concern in musical notation and printing, but they pose fewer problems for the conservator than do the conventions for indicating the durations of tones. A note typically consists of a notehead, which may be in outline (white) or filled in (black), and an ascending or descending stem, a short line that may have one or several flags attached. The duration of a note may be prolonged by a small dot following it; spaces where there is no sound are indicated by rests, the symbols for which are often quite small. Because music takes place in fixed time, it is essential that all these elements appear clearly; that they add up and balance each other properly. When notated music is reformatted, it is crucial that all this information be preserved. A loss of resolution that might seem minor in a printed text can make a musical score meaningless. If the center of a black note does not print, the performer will hold it too long; if a dot is lacking it will be too short. Musicians working from electrostatic copy often spend the first rehearsal pencilling over their music to make it legible.

Copyflow is particularly dangerous in this regard. An extreme case occurred when The New York Public Library sent a score of Scriabin's *Poeme d'Extase* for preservation in this manner. The reproduction, which alas was not noticed until years after the bound copy was put on the shelves, showed only tiny note heads scattered on blank sheets; everything else had vanished, stems, staves, notational symbols. What remained was an ironic reproduction of the earliest medieval notational system, "neumes in campo aperto," noteheads scattered in an empty field.

If musical notation were meant only to be read like a written text, the situation described above, though unusual, would not be crucial. But although the musically literate can read musical scores in their heads, this is not its principal purpose. Musical notation is primarily intended as a set of instructions to a performer, indicating what note or notes to produce in a given time frame. In addition, performance may involve other variable elements ranging from dynamics or repeats to such personal features as fingering, bowing, or "watch the conductor here!" (a pair of eyeglasses), which the performer customarily pencils into the working copy.

All of these instructions must be clearly visible while the performer is playing. Except in the case of singing, this will also involve an instrument that occupies a space between the performer and the page and engages the performer's hands as well. Be it for piano, clarinet, cello, or timpani, the necessity to see while playing, usually at a distance of two or more feet, is paramount in music for performance. Since the performer's hands are occupied, the music must also lie flat without assistance, and page turns may have to be executed at lightning speed. In some cases such as a marching band, one must also add portability to this list.

These two axiomatic requirements for music in performance —legibility at a distance and openability (if there is such a word) —give rise to an important corollary. Music, compared to books, comes in odd sizes. A standard score of 29 cm. is automatically oversize for most ordinary bookshelves. Most parts or sheet music are at least 33 cm. high; some 16th and 20th century volumes stand three feet tall. Undersize music is also commonplace; miniature study scores usually measure 18 cm.; librettos (literally "little books") of words to vocal music come in all shapes and sizes. Music for organ or for piano duet is customarily oblong and will stick far

10 MUSIC: WHY IS IT DIFFERENT?

out into the aisle of conventional shelving. Chamber, orchestral, and band parts are either loose sheets or virtually unbindable as they must be used on comparatively flimsy collapsible music stands. Solo sheet music, 14″ × 11″, and 10″ × 7″ choral music comes in units of three to five leaves. Scholarly editions in multi-volume bound sets are usually 17″ × 14″ in size.

Musical editions present all the paper problems common to libraries magnified. The international character of the art puts a great variety of paper on a music library's shelf. French paper is notoriously limp; German paper, stiff (both turn brittle). There is a further incentive to keep existing paper alive in music libraries. Music has a potentially longer active shelf life than most written texts if it can be kept in usable form. It is not uncommon for a first edition of Brahms to be in use today a hundred years after its publication, and we hope it may be in constant demand for another century.

We have noted the problems of legibility required for reformatting, the attention paid to noteheads, stems, dots, and staves, as well as size. (No, you can't perform from a microfilm). Binding is also affected by the need to keep music open. Oversewn volumes snap shut; perfect bindings fall apart; buckram is too heavy for a stand; spiral bindings, which work well in performance, are impossible on library shelves.

So there are some of the problems. What are music librarians doing about them? On a broader plane the Music Library Association together with its sister societies, the Association of Recorded Sound Collections (ARSC) and the International Association of Music Libraries, Archives, and Documentation Centres (IAML), have been active in addressing preservation topics. MLA has had a lively preservation committee for the past ten years whose interests have grown with those of the library preservation community as a whole. In 1984 the committee sponsored a pre-conference workshop focusing on hands-on solutions to local preservation problems. More recent national MLA meetings have included plenary sessions on preservation of music and sound recordings. The preservation committee regularly publishes a question and answer column "Lasting Concerns" in the *MLA Newsletter.* Music librarians have worked tirelessly to encourage music publishers to produce editions that will last. Through such groups as the joint committee of the Music Library Association and the Music Publishers Association great strides have been made in the production of bindable music and the use of acid-free paper. MLA's quarterly journal *Notes,* the most important reviewing and ordering tool in music, now identifies editions printed on acid-free paper with the standard infinity symbol as an incentive to buyers and publishers alike.

Music librarians have actively sought to raise consciousness of preservation concerns in the music community, in archives, orchestras, and schools as well as libraries. For example, one of the presentations you will hear later illustrates how one can explain archival preservation issues to a performing arts group with humor and style.

The other group we need to reach is the library community itself: administrators, conservators, etc. Our message to you is short. We, the music librarians, are ready to participate; in turn we need you to recognize our expertise and the special requirements needed so that we may work together successfully to preserve the rich musical heritage on our library shelves.

Working Against the Odds: Preservation Approaches in a Conservatory Library

Jane Gottlieb

ABSTRACT: A conservatory library has collections designed for use by performers. The art of performing is not passive, and the library material needs of performers are in many ways antithetical to the ideals of preservation. Performers require a closer engagement with the printed text and tend to be proprietary about the materials they use to create their art. The library collection is primarily designed for practical use by students and faculty. The first step in developing a preservation program is to articulate and understand its components: 1) the temperature, humidity, and light environments in which the collections are stored; 2) the physical means of housing the collections, or stacks and shelving arrangements; 3) systems for education of staff and patrons in proper care and handling of materials; 4) criteria for selection of materials for different types of preservation treatment; 5) access to collections and bibliographic control; and, 6) collection development policies that stipulate what materials will be discarded and replaced and what materials will be saved. At Juilliard the foundation for our preservation program was established by two different survey reports prepared by outside consultants. The next spark for accelerated development of the preservation program at Juilliard was the availability of state grant funding. In recent years, music librarians have been exploring preservation photocopying of deteriorated scores onto acid-free paper as an alternative to the expensive processes of microfilming or item-level conservation treatment. Reformatting materials by microfilming serves to preserve the informational content of the original. The temperature and humidity controls are part of the School's central HVAC system. Music librarians have been engaged in a fruitful dialogue with commercial binders over the years, and many binders have adopted proper standards for binding music materials. We recently had a condition survey of the circulating collection check factors of brittleness of paper, condition of binding, paper yellowing and tears, and presence of markings. 67.5% of the scores in the collection did not exhibit brittleness; 14.3% were somewhat brittle, and 18.2% were very brittle. Juilliard's collection is probably typical of collections of performance materials developed in this century in terms of the types of editions held.

Jane Gottlieb is Head Librarian at the Juilliard School in New York City. Ms. Gottlieb participates in the activities of METRO and serves on several preservation committees within that organization.

Conservatory libraries have collections designed for use by performers—at the Juilliard School this includes musicians, dancers and actors. The art of performing is not a passive one, and the library material needs of performers are in many ways antithetical to the ideals of preservation. Performers require a closer engagement with the printed text and tend to be proprietary about the materials they use to create their art. Their goal is to interpret the printed page for an audience. The text serves as the intermediary between what the composer wrote and their unique interpretation. It must be absorbed, devoured, and then transformed into a work of art: a transitory work of art, in fact, whose sounds and images will disappear unless recorded. Preservation work in a conservatory library, in a performance collection, involves understanding our users' needs and serving them while properly maintaining our collections, or, working against the odds.

The Juilliard School Library houses materials in all formats for our clientele. The collection includes ca. 47,000 scores, 18,000 books, 14,000 LP recordings, ca. 500 compact disc recordings and ca. 200 videos. In addition to these numbers in the fully cataloged collections, we also maintain ca. 18,000 scores and 14,000 LPs in organized storage collections.

The library also administers the School's Archives, ca. 554 cubic feet of administrative records, scrapbooks, photographs, and other materials documenting the history of the School since its founding in 1905. Finally, we house audio and video recordings of all Juilliard School performances: the recorded legacies of the School's current and former students, many of whom have achieved great prominence as performing artists.

The library collection is primarily designed for practical use by students and faculty; we do not attempt to duplicate the resources of a major research facility. We must provide ample resources to support undergraduate performance degrees in music, drama and dance, and graduate performance degrees in music.

Although at present we do not seek to acquire rare or special collection materials, we do happen to house ca. 1,200 rare items of various types, most of which were acquired through gifts to the School over the years. To describe our preservation program I will begin at the top, so to speak, by describing the preservation work accomplished on some of these special collection materials, much of which was supported by outside grant funding. In the course of working with these special collections we were forced to look more closely at the care of our circulating collections, and to develop a comprehensive collection management program realistically to care for library materials of all types.

Program Components

The first step in developing any type of "program" is to articulate and understand its components. This process is especially important in preservation work, in which so many variable factors must be considered and understood. These factors include the temperature, humidity, and light environments in which the collections are stored; the physical means of housing the collections, or stacks and shelving arrangements; systems for education of staff and patrons in proper care and handling of materials; criteria for selection of materials for different types of preservation treatment; access to collections and bibliographic control; and, collection development policies which stipulate what materials will be discarded and replaced and what materials will be saved (and at what cost).

None of these components of a preservation program can be viewed in a vacuum. It is important for library administrators to step back at times and view the larger picture, to articulate these concepts and understand how the various factors of preservation practice interact in their libraries. In music libraries we often talk about the "special needs" of our "special materials". However, it is important to remember that while the specifics of preservation practice are dictated by the format of the materials, the concepts of the practice are the same in all types of libraries.

SURVEY REPORTS

At Juilliard the foundation for our preservation program was established by two different survey reports prepared by outside consultants. The first survey was done in 1982 by John Townsend who is presently the administrator of the New York State Conservation/Preservation Program. John was one of the first graduates of the Columbia University Conservation Program, and his report provided practical information on proper environmental conditions and standard conservation procedures. The second report was commissioned from the Northeast Document Conservation Center in 1985. It required special institutional funding, which in itself was useful because the library's request helped to spark the School administration's awareness of the importance of preservation work.

Surveys or outside consultants' reports are useful in encouraging program development. Existing library staff members do not always have the time to prepare these types of reports, and outside consultants' documents often carry additional weight with administrators. We have, of course, all been warned not to trust everything that consultants tell us, but their reports can be quite helpful.

GRANT FUNDS

The next spark for accelerated development of the preservation program at Juilliard was the availability of state grant funding. Money is obviously a good incentive, although it is important to recognize that federal and state grant programs are usually designed to preserve materials of proven research value to a wide community, and are not geared to support ongoing collection management activities. The latter is the institution's own responsibility. New York was one of the first states to develop a preservation program. The New York State Discretionary Grant Program for the Conservation and Preservation of Library Research Materials was established in 1984. It "provides modest financial support (up to $25,000 per year) for projects that contribute to the preservation of significant research materials in libraries, archives, historical societies and other agencies within the State of New York, whether by conducting surveys, improving environments, and reformatting or treating collections."[1]

In addition to the discretionary grants, the New York State program provides annual preservation funding to eleven comprehensive research libraries in the state: Columbia, Cornell, The New York Public Library, The New York State Library, New York University, Syracuse University, The University of Rochester, and four State University of New York libraries. These eleven research libraries may in turn sponsor cooperative preservation grants.

Juilliard has several special collections that fit the state's criteria of having "significant research value." These include a collection of several hundred rare and early Liszt piano editions; ca. 450 nineteenth century librettos; Juilliard School archival materials such as scrapbooks, catalogs, etc.; and, 50 composers' manuscripts and 100 autograph letters. These materials had already been identified by the survey reports as candidates for preservation treatment (such as microfilming) that was not regularly supported by the general library budget.

The process of writing a grant application for funding by government agencies can and should be an educational experience. The first part of the educational experience of course is to consult with your institutional development office. It is very important to work closely with your institutional development office and gain their support for any library-specific funding projects you may wish to pursue. At Juilliard I am permitted to write applications for library-specific grants from government agencies. The development office handles all corporate and private donor fund raising activities. The New York State preservation grant application is quite specific in asking applicants to describe their existing preservation program, the collections to be preserved, how these collections fit in with the library's overall collection mission, and how preserved materials will be accessible to a wider community. Thus the process of writing such an application forces you to look closely at the collection and clearly justify the work to be done. The state is aware of the educational component of the grant application process, and in healthier budget years offered day-long workshops to assist applicants.

In all honesty I probably would not be here lauding the educational component of the grant-writing process if we had not also been successful in receiving funds. With support from the state program we have been able to microfilm the collection of early Liszt editions, the libretto collection, archival scrapbooks and publications, and the manuscript and letter collections. The state also supported rehousing and special conservation treatment for ca. 4,500 School performance photographs, and full scale conservation treatment (including deacidification) for 50 holograph scores.

In addition to the state grants for preservation work, in 1990 the library also received major funding from the National Historical Publications and Records Commission for a two-year Archives Development Project. The development of the archival program at Juilliard was certainly aided by the fact that we had already microfilmed and treated several of the archival collections with preservation grant funds.

Preservation Projects at Juilliard

What constitutes "special collections" in music? How, in fact, did we justify the "significant research value" of the collections to be preserved? The manuscript scores and autograph letters are of course unique documents. Our collection of these includes manuscripts of 2 Brahms songs: *Im Garten am Seegestade* (*The garden by the sea*), op. 70, no. 1 (1877) and *Sehnsucht* (*Longing*), op. 49, no. 3 (1868). Manuscripts of works by twentieth-century composers include several works commissioned by Juilliard, such as Leonard Bernstein's *Brass Music*, which was commissioned by the School in 1948.

Among the noteworthy items in our autograph collection are letters from Rossini, Saint-Saëns, Robert and Clara Schumann, and Richard Wagner's handwritten four-page critique of the first Königsberg performance of Bellini's *Norma* (1837).

Juilliard's Ruth Dana Collection of Liszt editions comprises several hundred early and first printed editions of the composer's music for solo piano. This collection is one of the largest single collections of early Liszt piano editions in this country. Liszt was an inveterate reviser of his compositions, and there are many significant differences to be found by studying the editions published within his lifetime. Many of the scores have decorative lithographed or engraved title pages, and are also interesting as exemplars of 19th century music publishing practices (see figure 1).

The Liszt collection was donated to the School in 1914 by the family of Ruth Dana Draper (1850–1914), an amateur pianist, and the mother of the monologist Ruth Draper (1884–1956). In 1969 the library requested special funding to have the collection rebound and treated by a professional conservator, who bleached the paper. As we know all too well, conservation approaches have changed since the late 1960s. The individual scores should not have been bound into thick volumes, both for bibliographic and conservation reasons, and bleaching paper can cause accelerated acidic damage.

In recent years, music librarians have been exploring preservation photocopying of deteriorated scores onto acid-free paper as an alternative to the expensive processes of microfilming or item-level conservation treatment.

Figure 1. Color lithographed title page of Liszt's piano arrangement of Ferdinand David's *Bunte Reihe* (or *Colored Series*): the title of each individual movement is printed on the different leaves. (Leipzig: Kistner, [1850]). Lithograph signed by Friedrich Kratzschmer.

Reformatting materials by microfilming serves to preserve the informational content of the original. Scholars are accustomed to studying microfilms, and paper copies can be generated from the film without further disturbing the original document. However, although the informational content of the original is preserved for all time, the format cannot be easily recreated. Paper copies generated via copy-flo or from a microfilm reader-printer must then be collated and bound into a format that resembles the original volume. In the case of music scores, the format of the material is inherent to its usability by performers.

Juilliard recently participated in a coordinated preservation photocopying project funded by the New York State grant program. Sponsored by New York University, the project also included the Music Division of the New York Public Library and Mannes College of Music. Each institution sent deteriorated scores from their collections to Booklab in Texas for preservation photocopying. The grant proposal made a clear case for the appropriateness of preservation photocopying as a cost-effective means for preserving music scores precisely because it produces surrogate copies of the original which can be utilized immediately by performers (see figures 2–6).

The copies produced at Booklab show almost all markings found on the originals, something that is not always the case on microfilms, where one struggles to determine whether the dark smudge on the page is an accidental or a smudge. These differences are obviously quite important when performing music.

Reformatting materials by preservation photocopying does not produce a permanent preservation copy (i.e., a microfilm master). Funding agencies are often reluctant to support re-formatting work that does not produce a microfilm master copy that can ultimately be shared by different libraries. However, it is important to recognize that preservation photocopying is a cost-effective process with many positive applications in music libraries. The Eastman School of Music in Rochester, NY, which houses the largest university music collection in this country, has reformatted many scores via photocopying as part of their preservation program. Since they have a microfilm facility on the premises, they can also make master microfilm copies of the materials. This is obviously the optimum approach to reformatting.

Figure 2. Piano-vocal scores of operas include the voice parts printed over a piano reduction of the orchestral parts. The scores are designed to lie flat when open on the piano stand.

The Commission on Preservation and Access, Cornell University, and the Xerox Corporation are currently involved in a joint digital scanning preservation project. Cornell is using Xerox software to scan, edit, store, catalog and print preservation copies of brittle items. We certainly look forward to a time when reformatting via digital scanning is cost-effective and available to many institutions as a preservation option.

The first conservation grant that we received in 1987 supported employment of a 10-hour-per-week conservation assistant. This position was designed for a student from the Columbia University Conservation Program. We have been fortunate to have the program in such close proximity (ca. 40 blocks away from Juilliard).[2] Conservation program students offer expertise that far

Figure 3. A piano-vocal score generated via copy-flo from a microfilm. It was bound along the longest edge, without any consideration of its use by the performer.

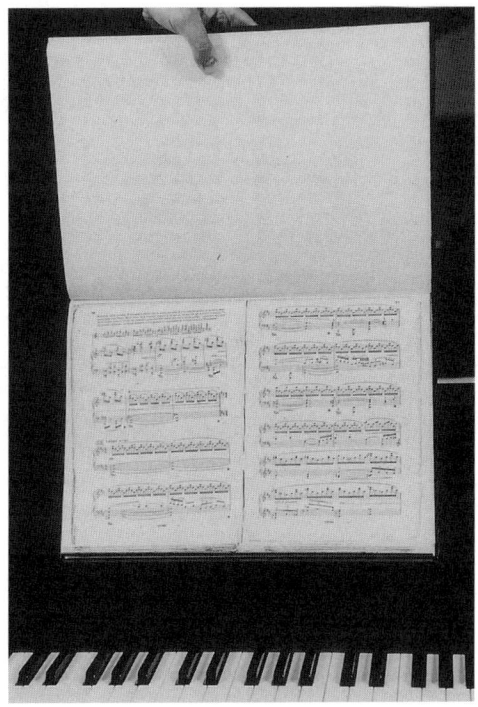

outweighs the amount they are paid per hour. Although this part-time position was initially grant-funded, it has since become a permanent library staff line: evidence of the institution's commitment to support an ongoing preservation program. We also have established a special budget line for the purchase of preservation supplies and materials.

Figure 4. Performer endeavoring to play from a piano-vocal score generated via copy-flo from a microfilm.

It is in these ways that the receipt of grant funds to preserve our "sexy" special collections helped to provide a solid foundation for an ongoing collection management program.

By 1991 we had successfully preserved many of the library's rare and special collections through microfilming, preservation photocopying, and special conservation treatment when appropriate. Under the supervision of the part-time conservation assistant the library staff also rehoused all of the rare materials in archival quality folders and boxes.

This work has been very satisfying, but collections do not remain static, and as stated above, one has to have a clear plan for managing the circulating collection.

24 WORKING AGAINST THE ODDS

Figure 5. A score before and after preservation photocopying (Corelli Sonatas from the Italian series *I Classici della musica Italiana*, Milan, 1918–1920).

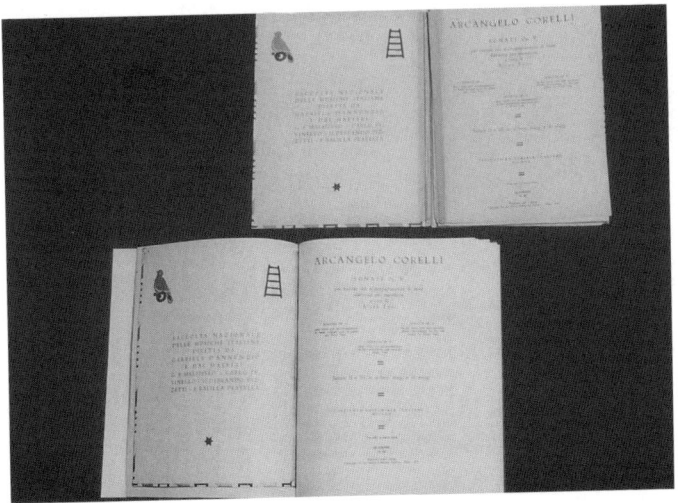

Environmental Considerations

The Juilliard School moved to its present home at Lincoln Center in 1969. The library was fairly well designed, with ample room for collection growth. It is two-tiered, with circulating scores on the first floor, the circulating book collection and the listening library on the second floor. The reference room includes a separate, walled-off cage area where the special collections are housed. Archival materials are also housed in segregated cage areas.

The temperature and humidity controls are part of the School's central HVAC system. We do monitor temperature and humidity and communicate problems to the building maintenance

Figure 6. A score before and after preservation photocopying (Corelli Sonatas from the Italian series *I Classici della musica Italiana*, Milan, 1918–1920). Booklab places the parts in separate acid-free enclosures bound into the volume.

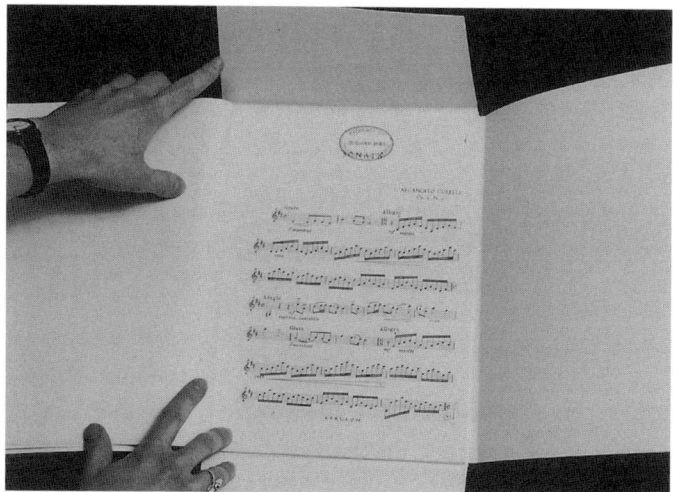

staff. However, as we all know, communicating problems does not always mean that change can be effected. In general, the environmental conditions are reasonably acceptable: during the last year our environmental monitoring showed an average relative humidity of 51% and temperature of 73 degrees F. The average temperature is slightly higher than the recommended 68 degrees F. We are also concerned about fluctuations in temperature and relative humidity caused by the fact that the central HVAC system is turned down over weekends. The problem of affecting changes in centralized environmental conditions is a difficult one for librarians. Building maintenance staffs are under pressure by high level administrators to keep air system costs down, and librarians' pleas for their collections are not always heeded. It is important to develop a good relationship with the building maintenance staff: to establish levels of mutual respect and credibility. Change is obviously easier to effect with open lines of communication. New York State has developed an "Environmental Control Resource Packet," which includes a report by William Lull and Paul Banks titled "Conservation Environment Guidelines for Libraries and Archives."[3] Mr. Lull is a building consultant and this report addresses all aspects of environmental controls to be considered when planning or renovating storage facilities. Designed for librarians and archivists, the document does not shy away from technical terms but rather serves to educate us to communicate more effectively about these matters. The Resource Packet is available from the New York State Library.[4]

Binding In-House

The Juilliard School library was also blessed with an in-house bindery, presently staffed by 1 full-time and 1 part-time bookbinder. We are thus able to exercise total control over binding work, and almost all scores are bound in-house.

This is indeed a blessing, because music requires special attention from bookbinders. Most importantly, the music must lie flat when opened: performers do not have extra sets of hands to hold the score open while playing from it.

Also, careful attention must be paid to the physical format of the work when preparing it for binding. The term "score" can refer to single-entity scores, such as conductor scores or study scores (miniature or full-size), and sets of parts, or even scores and parts, which must be housed together for distribution to all members of an ensemble. Publishers issue music in all of these formats, and libraries must be careful to bind them for usability.

For example, piano trios are usually issued as 3 parts: the piano "score" (which also includes cue notes for the violin and 'cello), and separate parts for the violinist and 'cellist. The piano score is invariably thicker than the other 2 parts, and a common binding approach is to sew the piano part into the binding and place the other parts in a separate pocket.

This method is problematic, however, when used for parts of equal size, such as the four parts of a string quartet. In this case, sewing one part (usually the first violin part) into the binding and placing the other three parts in the pocket produces an inordinate weight on the first violin part. A preferable approach when the parts are of equal size is to bind each part separately and then place them in pockets.

UNUSUAL SCORE FORMATS

These are standard formats of performance materials found in most music collections. Many twentieth-century scores and avant garde works are issued in more unusual formats: composers do not necessarily think about the storage and housing needs of their creations. Displayed on the exhibit table is a copy of Stockhausen's *Klavierstücke XI, nr. 7*, a chance composition that was issued by the publisher in a cardboard tube with a wooden stand for mounting the music so that the pianist could view the entire page at once. The exhibit copy is from the New York Public Library collection: they retained the cardboard tube and the wooden stand, while at Juilliard we placed our copy of the same work in a custom made case, which is the standard housing we use for works with individual leaves which cannot be sewn into a binding (figure 7).

Another example of a problematic twentieth-century work is the score of Ligeti's *Trio* for violin, horn and piano (Schott, 1984). The published score is a facsimile of the composer's manuscript. Mr. Ligeti suggests that the players cut the pages along the dotted lines

28 WORKING AGAINST THE ODDS

Figure 7. Juilliard copy of Stockhausen's *Klavierstücke XI, nr. 7* (Universal, 1957). Performing Directions: "the performer looks at random at the sheet of music and begins with any group, the first that catches his eye..."

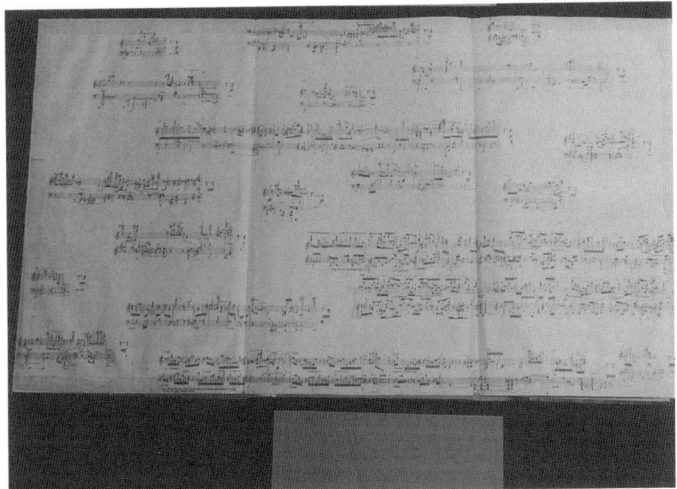

printed near the margins so the pages can be moved around easily on the music stand. Of course, if the players follow his directions, the library will be left with an empty binding!

Contemporary composers also tend to be fond of oversize formats, which require space for housing these larger than 42 cm. giants. Spiral bindings (the bane of librarians) are also popular formats for facsimiles of composers' manuscripts. Music librarians have been engaged in a fruitful dialogue with commercial binders over the years, and many binders have adopted proper standards for binding music materials.[5]

PAPER CONDITION

We recently had a condition survey of the circulating collection done by Elizabeth Sadewhite.[6] She sampled 151 scores checking factors of brittleness of paper, condition of binding, paper yellowing and tears, and presence of markings. The results of this survey are quite interesting, especially in the area of paper brittleness: 67.5% of the scores in the collection did not exhibit brittleness; 14.3% were somewhat brittle, and 18.2% were very brittle. This last figure is very close to the percentage of brittle scores found in the music collection at Yale University: a condition survey done there in the early 1980s revealed that 17% of the scores in their collection were very brittle.[7]

Juilliard's collection is probably typical of collections of performance materials developed in this century in terms of the types of editions held. The paper used by French and German publishers tends to be quite brittle, with the French publications being slightly worse than the German ones.

Maintenance Decision-Making

So how does one manage to maintain a heavily-used collection with so many materials that have relatively short shelf lives? Some of our preservation decisions are conscious actions of "benign neglect", or, as we abbreviate it: "let die (LD)". A more common phrase used by many libraries for the same treatment is phased deterioration (sometimes abbreviated as PHD). We need to have enough copies of standard repertoire works in different editions available for circulation. Without unlimited funds for replacement copies, we try to recycle usable materials as long as possible. However, you also have to know what can be replaced, either with the same edition or a reprint of that particular edition. It is important to realize that music editions are in themselves quite distinctive, and there can be many variations in different editions of the same work. Some are edited by famous performers, while others are supposed to be "urtext," and educated performers will "edition shop" carefully. For example, we presently list 20 different editions of Beethoven piano sonatas in our catalog; 3 of these editions are out-of-print and kept in the cage collection (figure 8).

Reprint editions of music scores are quite common, and of course vary in quality themselves. A reprint score may not reveal what edition it is a reprint of.

Of course music editions which cannot be replaced should be removed for preservation photocopying or re-housing before they disintegrate beyond salvation. Thus all preservation decisions must involve the collection manager and/or acquisitions librarian.

In recent years the Music Library Association has been working closely with the Music Publishers Association to encourage the use of acid-free paper. We have been quite successful in convincing many of the U.S. publishing houses to use better quality paper, and of late even some of the Europeans have come around.

Education of users is a very important part of any preservation program, and especially crucial in a performance collection. At Juilliard all first-year students are given library tours during which basic library rules and procedures are explained. We ask them always to bring library materials in need of repair to the attention of a staff member, and not to attempt basic repair themselves. They are also asked not to put pencil (or pen) markings in library materials. It becomes evident to anyone browsing through the score collection in The Juilliard School library that this latter rule is impossible to enforce in performance collections.

Ms. Sadewhite's survey revealed that 35.1% of the scores sampled were slightly marked, and 7.8% heavily marked. Pencil markings indicating phrasing are, in many performer's views, a necessary aspect of their absorption of a musical work, whether the

Illustration no. 8. The first page of Beethoven's *Appassionata Sonata* (no. 23, op. 57) from 4 different editions. It is evident that the 4 editors have taken very different approaches to the presentation and interpretation of the same music. These differences are more significant for the reading of the work than the variations found in, for example, different editions of *Huckelberry Finn* or the novels of Edith Wharton.

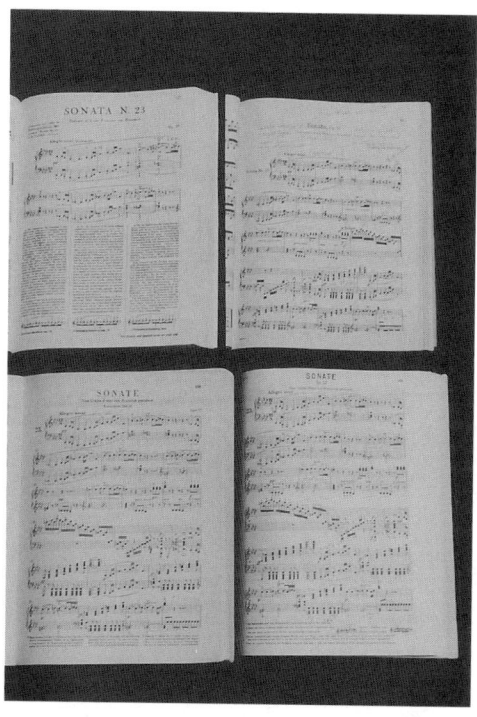

score is their own or the library's. Even if the students are deterred from marking scores, they can't always stop their teachers from entering phrase markings. We have many renowned faculty members who unabashedly come into the library looking for the particular score they have marked up. And then the question of the importance of these markings arises. We have scores in special collections that are there precisely because they include some famous performer's markings.

I have focused most of my comments on the score collection to show some of the "special problems" of preserving printed music materials in a conservatory library. Jerry Gibson has addressed the problems of preserving recorded sound materials on today's panel.

At Juilliard, the recording collection does not circulate. LPs are housed on open shelves; CDs, cassettes, and reel-to-reel tapes in closed stack areas. Students must present their ID card in exchange for a key which turns on the power at a listening station.

The record librarian and her staff exercise excellent supervision over the facility, and we honestly do not have serious problems with user damage to recordings. LP recordings are cleaned daily using a VPI record cleaner system and disc cleanser solution. Like everyone else we have no choice but to purchase CDs almost exclusively these days, and the recent awareness of their relatively short life-spans (5 to 8 years?) is sobering to say the least.

We are concerned about preserving the reel-to-reel tape and acetate recordings of Juilliard School performances. Our archive of School performances began in 1950, and most of the reel-to-reel tape recordings have reached their 25 to 30 year lifespan. The problem of preserving sound recordings in music schools and conservatories is one that would benefit from a national coordinated effort. While most of our recorded performances are primarily of local importance, they become of interest to a wider community when our students have attained careers as world-class performers, or when the works recorded are premieres. The Juilliard School has commissioned and premiered many significant works in our 86-year history, and some of our archival tapes document unique performances of particular works.

There has recently been a lot of activity in the archival and sound recording circles on the problems of preserving sound recordings. This past week (June 24–28) the Peabody Conservatory of Music in Baltimore hosted a workshop on "Audio Transfer Technology for the Sound Archivist" sponsored by the Audio Engineering Society Preservation Committee and the Associated Audio Archives committee of the Association for Recorded Sound Collections (ARSC). The 1990 meeting of the Society of American Archivists in Seattle included a session on this same problem titled "Sound of Silence," the proceedings of which will be published in an upcoming issue of *Midwestern Archivist*.[8] It is crucial that librarians stay in touch with these events sponsored by other professional organizations. The problems of preserving our recorded legacies are complex: the equipment needed for proper tape preservation is expensive and often out of reach of small conservatories and music schools. However, our recorded legacies are quickly disappearing, and we must educate ourselves and work together to preserve what we can.

Similarly, the School has been documenting opera and drama performances on video since 1988. The master tapes are housed in the recording department, and use copies are housed in the library. The Dance Division has been documenting its performances on film and later video since their beginnings in 1951. Juilliard's Dance Division has a distinguished history. Among the founding faculty members were choreographers José Limón, Anthony Tudor, Martha Graham, and Doris Humphrey. Many of the School's performances were premieres of works by these choreographers, and our film and video archive represents an important national resource.

I hope that in describing the preservation program at The Juilliard School I have shed some light on the administrative and practical approaches to preservation in a performance collection.

We must care for our library materials in their special formats and our users with their special needs; and, all of this must be done with an eye towards documenting our performance histories as they are made.

Notes and References

1. The New York State Program for the Conservation and Preservation of Library Research Materials, *Discretionary Grant Guidelines and Application* (Albany, NY: New York State Library Division of Library Development), pg. 1.

2. The Columbia University Conservation Program was part of the School of Library Service, which closed in the Spring of 1992; the Conservation Program moved to the University of Texas at Austin earlier that year.

3. William Lull with Paul F. Banks, "Conservation Environment Guidelines for Libraries and Archives," *Environmental Control Resource Packet* (Albany, NY: The New York State Library, 1991).

4. The *Environmental Control Resource Packet* can be ordered from the Conservation/Preservation Program Office, New York State Library Division of Library Development, 10-C-47 Cultural Education Center, Albany, NY 12230; tel: (518) 474-6971.

5. See Ted Honea, "Music . . . A Binding Challenge." *New Library Scene* 4, no. 3 (June 1985): 1, 8–10.

6. The author is grateful to Elizabeth Sadewhite for permission to use this information.

7. Gay Walker et al., "The Yale Survey: A Large-Scale Study of Book Deterioration in the Yale University Library," *College and Research Libraries* 46 (March 1985): 111–132.

8. *Midwest Archivist* 16, no. 1 (Spring 1991).

A Condition Survey of the Circulating Score Collection of the Juilliard School

Elizabeth Sadewhite

ABSTRACT: The circulating score collection in The Juilliard School Library was a useful subject for a study of condition of scores in a music library. The survey was conducted at The Juilliard School in 1991—154 of 160 items were surveyed. The resulting data were entered into a file in SPSS/PC+ Studentware for statistical study. The most eye-catching crosstabulation was that of country of origin and brittleness—French very brittle percentages were far higher than any others, and the German nearly twice as high as the rest. Brittle paper did not prevent the circulation of a score. In 1990–91 the circulation rate for brittle items was lower than that for non-brittle, but still 25.9% of the very brittle scores had circulated in that year. The two doublefold brittleness test yielded 18.2%—lower than Yale but higher than Syracuse. The primary aim of the survey was to determine the condition of the collection, but it was irresistible to try to see whether those results were dependent on one or more descriptive variables. The implications for collection maintenance are tantalizing. However, the size of the sample was too small to generate reliable chi-square tests for many variables, the date of publication or manufacture impossible to determine, and the circulation data incomplete.

In 1981, Sara Buchanan and Sandra Coleman reported on the book condition survey of the Green Library at Stanford University performed in 1971.[1] One of the first such studies of an academic library, it was inspired by the current concerns about paper embrittlement. Three elements were considered and graded: paper, binding, and cover. A weighted average reflecting the importance of the paper was recorded for each of 400 books, yielding the result

---

At the time of this survey Elizabeth D. Sadewhite was a student at the Columbia University School of Library Service and a part-time music cataloger at The Juilliard School. She thanks Richard Smiraglia, then Assistant Professor of the former, and Jane Gottlieb, Head Librarian of the latter, for their help in the preparation of this paper.

that 26.5% of the books were in poor condition. Several surveys more or less closely following the Stanford model have been conducted at other university libraries in the United States in the last decade, most notably the large-scale study at Yale.[2] However, to date there has been no survey focusing exclusively on printed music. As a student of music librarianship at Columbia University and a part-time cataloger at The Juilliard School, I was curious to see whether such a study would yield results similar to those of the more general surveys.

The circulating score collection in The Juilliard School Library was a useful subject for this study. Founded in 1905, the collection of ca. 47,000 volumes contains a comprehensive selection of editions printed in the late 19th and 20th centuries. The survey discussed in this paper was performed to determine the extent of the brittle book syndrome in the collection and to see whether any of the results could be attributed to special characteristics of printed music.

Reports of the Stanford, Yale, Syracuse,[3] and Illinois[4] surveys were reviewed to determine which variables might be appropriate for a survey of the circulating score collection at Juilliard. The Yale study was of particular interest because it was stratified by library. The Yale music library was surveyed as a separated entity, and although the sample included both books and printed music, the results were expected to be especially relevant to this study.

Because of limitations of time and personnel, the basic Stanford model (condition of cover, binding, and paper, the last of these of the greatest interest) was adopted with a few additional variables that were hoped would prove to be significant, or at least of interest, for a study of printed music. Markings, pencil, and other, were noted. Mutilation had been mentioned as a particular problem in the music collection at Yale (musicians are often taught from the first lesson to mark their parts, preferably in pencil). One of the special requirements of printed music is that it lie flat when opened. This characteristic is largely dependent on the binding, so the type of binding and the number of signatures were noted. Because scores can vary so tremendously in extent (from a one- or two- page song to an eight-hundred page score), the number of pages was also recorded. The collection to be surveyed is a *circulating* collection, so whether an item had ever circulated and the last date of circulation (date due) were included. The extent of previous repair also seemed to be easily recognizable and potentially informative.

As in other surveys, the survey identification number, call number, title, and place of publication were recorded. The publisher was included as well, for multiple manifestations of the same work are more common in the case of musical scores than in that of books.

One of the more awkward characteristics of printed music is the common absence of a publication date. In the Juilliard survey, one variable was assigned to copyright date and another to accession or cataloging date with the hope that one or the other would be present but with the fear that there would be many missing values.

The Juilliard School Library presently uses a manual circulation system. A pocket is glued into each item to hold a card which is removed at the time of circulation and affixed with a sticker printed with the identification of the patron and the date due. The card is then filed as a surrogate for the item. Upon return of the item, the sticker is discarded. Each book or score also contains a slip that is stamped with the date due; when filled, the slip is removed and a new one glued in. Therefore, all that can be reliably deduced from an item on the shelf is whether it has ever circulated (even with a new date-due slip it is possible to tell whether the circulation card has ever had a date-sticker attached), and, in most cases, its last date due.

38 A CONDITION SURVEY

A pilot survey was performed to derive an estimate of the potential proportion of brittle items. 16.66% of the items were brittle. That figure was used in the following formula to determine sample size:

$$n = \frac{z^2 Np(1-p)}{NE^2 + z^2 p(1-p)}$$

n = sample size
z = curve value for confidence interval 90% (1.65)
N = total population in sampling frame (47,000)
P = expected proportion of brittle items (16.66%)
E = tolerable error = -5%

The resulting minimum number of items to be sampled is 151.

The scores for the final survey were selected from the shelf list. Pairs of random numbers generated by computer determined first the drawer and then the location of the card within that drawer by its distance from the front in centimeters. If the second number yielded a result beyond the last card in the drawer, that pair of numbers was discarded. If the designated card was not the first of a set, that pair of numbers was discarded. In order to compensate for the difference in the thicknesses of cards, Fussler's sampling technique was used.[5] The third card behind the actual card measured was chosen. The next, or in the case of the last, the first, drawer was considered a continuation if one of the last three cards in the drawer was drawn.

The survey was conducted at The Juilliard School on April 13, 17, 20, and 22, 1991. One anticipated problem, the unavailability of certain items for examination, proved to be very minor: 154 of 160 items were easily located and surveyed. The resulting data were entered into a file in SPSS/PC+ Studentware for statistical study.

Survey Results

DESCRIPTIVE VARIABLES

Call # (Classification)

At Juilliard a modified Dickinson classification system for scores is used. Although the sample was not stratified, the frequency table for classification should be closely related to the actual distribution of scores in the library. Many interesting observations could probably be made combining classification with other variables, e.g. latest circulation, condition of binding, brittleness, etc.; however, the frequencies for each class were too small to yield statistically significant results in crosstabulations. When the classes were recorded into larger groups, some interesting trends began to appear (last circulation date, country of origin, and pencil markings all began to look class-dependent), but the expected frequencies in chi-square tests were often below five more than 50% of the time, rendering the results unreliable. A much larger sample would have to be drawn to note significant differences between groupings like string and wind music or full-size and miniature scores.

Country Of Publication

Because of the size of the sample, the publication was not coded for city. If more than one country was named, the most prominent was used. The United States ranked first with 47.4%, followed in descending order by Germany (East and West combined) at 20.1%, England, 13.0%, France, 11.7%, Austria, 5.8%, and Italy, Poland, and the U.S.S.R. tied for last at .6% each (the equivalent of one observation). The last three were combined into one category, 'Other,' for convenience in tabulation (see figure 1).

Figure 1. Country of Publication

Value Label	Value	Frequency	Percent	Valid Percent	Cum Percent
U.S.	1	73	47.4	47.4	47.4
Eng.	2	20	13.0	13.0	60.4
Fra.	3	18	11.7	11.7	72.1
Ger.	4	31	20.1	20.1	92.2
Aus.	6	9	5.8	5.8	98.1
Other	9	3	1.9	1.9	100.0
	Total	154	100.0	100.0	

Valid Cases   154   Missing Cases   0

Copyright Date

As anticipated, there were many missing copyright values. Forty (26%) of the cases had no publisher-supplied date of any sort. When collapsed into categories by decade a general trend appears: a gradual increase from the turn of the century to 1970, then a decrease for the '80's.

Accession/Cataloging Date

In an attempt to provide a date for all scores, this variable was chosen as a possible alterative to copyright. Unfortunately it, too, had many missing values (34 or 22.1%). Also, it was discovered during the survey that the date was not recorded with any regularity on items cataloged before 1960. Any trend indicated by the frequency table of collapsed categories is really a result of library practice rather than a record of the age of the collection.

Number of Pages

This variable, ranging from 3 to 869, certainly shows some of the extremes possible in score collections. Nearly two thirds (65.5%) of the scores had 64 or fewer pages (figure 2).

Figure 2. Number of Pages

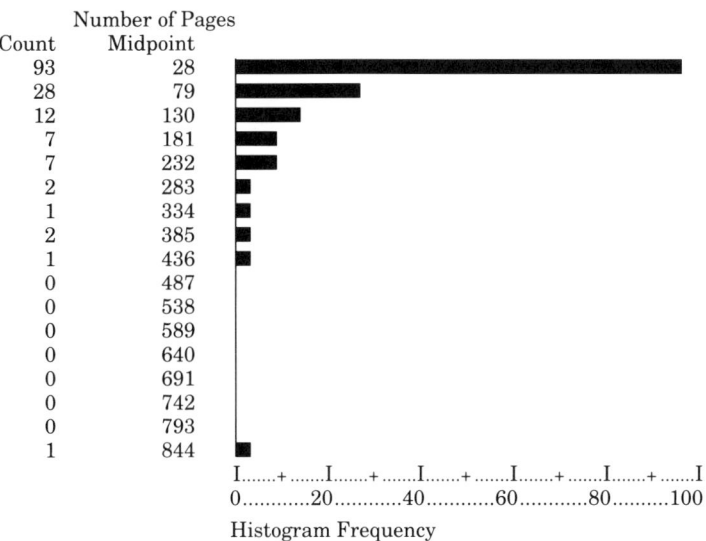

Signatures

Single signature scores make up the largest group at 57.6% with 6 or more (24.7%) the only other category exceeding single digits. The number of signatures was useful in combination with binding variables.

Origin of Binding

The scores were nearly all bound either inhouse or at a commercial bindery; only 3.9% had original publisher's bindings. This is not a surprising result, because printed music is commonly sold with a soft cover, and, if it has a single signature, attached with staples.

Binding Construction

The overwhelming majority (94.8%) of the scores in the survey sample were sewn all-along. Loose sheets made up 1.9%, oversewn and adhesive another 1.9%, and adhesive alone or Pambind each occurred just once (.6%).

Year of Last Circulation

Although this is not an entirely reliable variable (it seems likely that some change in library date-due stamping rather than actual fact caused the remarkable gap between 1969 and 1981), the dates in the eighties were stamped consistently. The statistics for these years show that the collection is heavily used (figure 3). Over 60% of the sample scores were circulated in the last five years, and over 75% in the last decade. Twenty items (13% of the sample) had never been circulated.

Publisher was not coded. *Number of Parts* was coded but not used beyond a classification distribution.

CONDITION VARIABLES

All condition variables are displayed in figure 4.

Cover

The condition of the cover of a score is probably an indication of use, or at least of wear. 45.5% of the sampled scores had covers in good condition, 40.9% showed some wear, and 13.6% were in need of repair. These statistics would be interesting to compare with real circulation data.

Condition of Binding

This was the only binding variable with several values large enough to make it interesting. 56.5% of the sampled scores had

Figure 3. Year of Last Circulation

Last circulation grouped into categories

Value Label	Value	Frequency	Percent	Valid Percent	Cum Percent
1990–1991	1	58	37.7	38.4	38.4
1987–1989	2	53	21.4	21.9	60.3
1984–1986	3	17	11.0	11.3	71.5
1981–1983	4	6	3.9	4.0	75.5
Before 1980	5	17	11.0	11.3	86.8
Never circulated	6	20	13.0	13.2	100.0
	9	3	1.9	MISSING	
	Total	154	100.0	100.0	

Valid Cases   151   Missing Cases   3

Figure 4. Condition Variables

	0 Good (None)	1 Fair (Minor)	2 Poor (Major)
Cover	70 45.5%	63 40.9%	21 13.6%
Binding	87 56.5%	41 26.6%	26 16.9%
Paper			
Brittle	104 67.5%	22 14.3%	28 18.2%
Yellow	54 35.1%	76 49.4%	24 15.6%
Torn	100 64.9%	29 18.8%	25 16.2%
Markings			
Pencil	88 57.1%	54 35.1%	12 7.8%
Other	143 92.9%	9 5.8%	2 1.3%
Previous repair	128 83.1%	17 11.0%	9 5.8%

bindings in excellent or good condition, 26.6% were in fair condition, and 16.9% were in poor condition. Binding condition would also seem to be an indication of wear; it cries out to be compared with circulation data.

The next three variables concern paper, the chief focus of most condition surveys. New covers and bindings are useless if the paper is fundamentally unsound.

Paper Yellowing

The assignment of this value required a particularly subjective judgement on the part of the surveyor. There is a great range of color in paper even when new, so unless the paper is still absolutely white, the amount of yellowing can be at best an educated guess, at worst a shot in the dark. Therefore the 35.1%, 49.4%, and 15.6% figures for not yellowed to very yellow were not used in many tabulations. They did, however, correlate closely to brittleness. It would be very interesting to cross tabulate yellowing with date variables, but, as described above, the latter were also problematic.

Torn Paper

The percentages closely mirror the brittleness results, though they are a little higher in the middle category of minor rips (18.8%) and lower in the extreme range: major tears that obscure the intellectual content or truly hinder use (16.2%) (pages must be able to be turned quickly and surely in performance). 64.9% of the paper was not torn.

Pencil Markings

Resulting from another subjective choice, 57% of the scores had no markings, 35.1% were judged slightly marked, and 7.8%

heavily marked (enough to be distracting). The high percentages in the last two categories was expected for printed music. A cross tabulation with classification is included (figure 5).

Other Markings

The percentage of the surveyed items marked with something other than the erasable pencil was much lower: 5.8% slightly marked and 1.3% heavily marked. The two markings variables overlapped; all but 3 (1.9% of total sample) of the scores with other markings were also marked with pencil.

Previous Repair

The largest part of the sample had received no previous repair (83.1%) while 11% had minor repairs (one or two pieces of Japanese tissue or pressure tape) and 5.8% major repairs. These statistics were interesting when combined with brittleness and might have some correlation with class or circulation figures (figure 6).

Some Conclusions

The most eye-catching crosstabulation was that of country of origin and brittleness (figure 7). The French very brittle percentages were far higher than any others, and the German nearly twice as high as the rest. The observation values were low, yet several t-tests seemed warranted (figure 8). When comparing the United States and France, the probability that the null hypothesis was true was less than .005. In a test comparing the German and U.S. means, the probability of .059 is still quite low. It is hardly news to most musicians that French printed music does not hold up well, and it is good to have evidence in black and white.

Figure 5. Pencil Markings

	Mean	Std. Dev.	Cases
Piano	.7576	.7513	33
Organ	.2000	.4472	5
Strings and winds	.6471	.6063	17
Instrumental chamber	.3636	.5045	11
Solo voice	.5500	.6048	20
Instrumental scores	.4722	.6964	36
Vocal scores	.3810	.4976	21
Libretti	.0000	.0000	8
Folk songs	.3333	.5774	3
Total	.5065	.6391	154

Figure 6. Previous Repair

Crosstabulation: Previous repair By Paper brittleness

Count Row Pct	Not brittle 0	Somewhat brittle 1	Very brittle 2	Row Total
No previous repairs 0	98 76.6	15 11.7	15 11.7	128 83.1
Minor repairs 1	3 17.6	7 41.2	7 41.2	17 11.0
Major repairs 2	3 33.3		6 66.7	9 5.8
Column Total	104 67.5	22 14.3	28 18.2	154 100.0

Number of Missing Observations = 0

It was interesting to note that brittle paper did not prevent the circulation of a score. In 1990–91 the circulation rate for brittle items was lower than that for non-brittle, but still 25.9% of the very brittle scores had circulated in that year. This has implications for the necessity of replacing the brittle items, especially since

Figure 7. Country of Origin and Brittleness

Summaries of By levels of		Paper brittleness Country of publication		
	Label	Mean	Std. Dev.	Cases
		.5065	.7859	154
	U.S.	.3699	.6974	73
	Eng.	.4000	.6806	20
	Fra.	1.1111	.9003	18
	Ger.	.6774	.8713	31
	Aus.	.2222	.6667	9
	Other	.0000	.0000	3

Total Cases = 154

Crosstabulation:			Paper brittleness By Country of publication				
	Count Col Pct		U.S. 1	Eng. 2	Fra. 3	Ger. 4	Aus. 6	Row Total
Not brittle	0	55 75.3	14 70.0	6 33.3	18 58.1	8 88.9	101 66.9
Somewhat brittle	1	9 12.3	4 20.0	4 22.2	5 16.1		22 14.6
Very brittle	2	9 12.3	2 10.0	8 44.4	8 25.8	1 11.1	28 18.5
	Column Total	73 48.3	20 13.2	18 11.9	31 20.5	9 6.0	151 100.0

Number of Missing Observations = 0

it became clear that they were at high risk when circulated. Uncirculated very brittle items were only slightly ripped, while 75% of recently circulated (last 5 years) very brittle items fell into the extreme torn paper category (figure 9).

In the music library stratum of the Yale survey, the two double-fold brittleness test yielded a very similar 17% (this was the

Figure 8. T-tests

Independent samples of Country of publication
t-test for: Paper brittleness

	Number of Cases	Mean	Standard Deviation	Standard Error
U.S.	73	.3699	.697	.082
France	18	1.1111	.900	.212

F Value	2-Tail Prob.	Pooled Variance Estimate			Separate Variance Estimate		
		t Value	Degrees of Freedom	2-Tail Prob.	t Value	Degrees of Freedom	2-Tail Prob.
1.67	.140	−3.80	89	.000	−3.26	22.29	.004

Independent samples of Country of publication
t-test for: Paper brittleness

	Number of Cases	Mean	Standard Deviation	Standard Error
U.S.	73	.3699	.697	.082
Germany	31	.6774	.871	.156

F Value	2-Tail Prob.	Pooled Variance Estimate			Separate Variance Estimate		
		t Value	Degrees of Freedom	2-Tail Prob.	t Value	Degrees of Freedom	2-Tail Prob.
1.56	.128	−1.91	102	.059	−1.74	47.09	.088

entire music collection of circulating and non-circulating books and scores) to Juilliard's circulating score 18.2%. This is considerably lower than the Yale 28.9% overall average but higher than the Syracuse 12.2%. In this study it is not possible to draw any conclusions from these percentages or offer any explanations. Perhaps the age of the collections is a factor. It would be interesting to compare the paper stock of books and scores in a future study. The Yale mutilation cannot strictly be compared with the Juilliard markings,

Figure 9. Circulation and Brittleness

Crosstabulation: Last circulation grouped in categories
By Paper brittleness

	Count Col Pct	Not brittle 0	Somewhat brittle 1	Very brittle 2	Row Total
1990–1991	1	43 42.2	8 36.4	7 25.9	58 38.4
1987–1989	2	25 24.5	3 13.6	5 18.5	33 21.9
1984–1986	3	10 9.8	3 13.6	4 14.8	17 11.3
1981–1983	4	3 2.9	2 9.1	1 3.7	6 4.0
Before 1980	5	7 6.9	4 18.2	6 22.2	17 11.3
Never circulated	6	14 13.7	2 9.1	4 14.8	20 13.2
	Column Total	102 67.5	22 14.6	27 17.9	151 100.0

Number of Missing Observations = 3

because the Yale variable included more than marking, but the 44.8% total of items with pencil and other markings at Juilliard certainly justified the assumption that the figure would be high.

In this survey, there were two distinct groups of variables, those that describe and identify the item which was put on the shelf, and those that are mutable through use and the passage of time. The primary aim of the survey was to determine the condition of the collection, but it was irresistible to try to see whether those results were dependent on one or more of the first variables, on some intrinsic characteristic of the item. Then, because the collection studied circulates, circulation data, as far as they were available, were put to use in an attempt to view the results from another angle. With more complete circulation data, a whole range of relationships could be discovered. The implications for collection maintenance are tantalizing. However, the size of the sample (after all, it was determined using the anticipated percentage of brittle paper) was too small to generate reliable chi-square tests for many variables, the date of publication or manufacture impossible to determine, and the circulation data incomplete. The study was, however, a start, a beginning to the story, and perhaps some future surveyors will continue the tale.

References

1. Sara Buchanan and Sandra Coleman, "Deterioration Survey of the Stanford University Libraries Green Library Stack Collection." In *Preservation Planning Program Resource Notebook*, comp. Pamela W. Darling, p. 189–221 (Washington, D.C.: Association of Research Libraries, Office of Management Studies, 1987).

2. Gay Walker et al., "The Yale Survey: A Large-Scale Study of Book Deterioration in the Yale University Library" *College & Research Libraries* 46:111–132.

3. Randall Bond et al., "Preservation Study at the Syracuse University Libraries" *College & Research Libraries* 48:132–147.

4. Tina Chrzastowski et al., "Library Collection Deterioration: A study at the University of Illinois at Urbana-Champaign" *College & Research Libraries* 50:577–584.

5. Abraham Bookstein, "Sampling from Card Files" *Library Quarterly* 53 (1988): 310–311)

Mass Deacidification at the Northwestern University Music Library

Kenneth Calkins

> **ABSTRACT:** Mass deacidification is a highly efficient preservation technology. At Northwestern University, vapor-phase deacidification has been applied to the circulating music collection. This ongoing program is described with regard to selection, processing, quality assurance, and treatment costs. A summary of diethyl zinc (DEZ) vapor treatment is provided.

Background

Research library collections face imminent devastation from paper acidity. Most paper manufactured since the mid nineteenth century contains ingredients that promote acid formation. Acid progressively weakens cellulose fibers, causing the paper to become brittle and unusable. Acidic paper will self-destruct in as soon as fifty years. Only in recent years have a growing number of publishers switched to alkaline paper. The trend toward alkaline paper is confined to North American publishers. Foreign publishers with little exception continue to use acidic paper.

Preservation options for acidic materials include reformatting to microfilm or photocopy. However, reformatting is generally not considered to be cost-effective for large numbers of volumes and

---

Kenneth Calkins is the Recorded Sound Services Librarian at Northwestern University. Previously he worked at the Rodgers & Hammerstein Archives of Recorded Sound of The New York Public Library for the Performing Arts, first as Cataloger/Archivist and then as Chief Cataloger/Reference Librarian. This paper is an expanded version of an article that appeared in the "Lasting Concerns" column of the *MLA Newsletter* 93 (May-June 1993): 6. The author wishes to acknowledge the assistance of Elayne Bond of the Northwestern University Library Preservation Department.

it is inappropriate for materials with enduring value in the original format. In response to the urgency and extent of the acidic paper problem, in the 1970's the Library of Congress began experimental research for a practical method to deacidify large numbers of volumes *en masse*.[1] In collaboration with Akzo Chemicals, a unique mass deacidification technology was developed that uses a vapor rather than a liquid. The compound diethyl zinc (DEZ) in vapor phase penetrates the pages of a closed volume to neutralize existing acids in the paper. DEZ also deposits an alkaline reserve that guards against future acid formation.[2]

Akzo Chemicals now holds the license for the DEZ process. The other mass deacidification technology currently available commercially is a liquid treatment developed by the FMC Corporation.[3] In December, 1993, Akzo Chemicals announced termination of their mass deacidivication services by April, 1994, for financial reasons. The Preservation Department of the Northwestern University Library has since been actively investigating other vendors now marketing alternative technologies.

The Northwestern University Library became actively involved with mass deacidification in 1989 through participation in a project conducted by the Committee on Institutional Cooperation (CIC), a consortium of twelve midwestern universities (Indiana, Michigan State, Northwestern, Ohio State, Pennsylvania State, and Purdue Universities, and the Universities of Chicago, Illinois, Iowa, Michigan, Minnesota, and Wisconsin). CIC library directors charged a task force to investigate the chemical treatment and organizational issues of a mass deacidification program. Test runs served as the primary means for investigation.[4]

The CIC task force completed its report in April, 1992. Two months later, Northwestern signed with Akzo for DEZ treatment services. Although the task force report established the need for mass deacidification among the CIC libraries, the CIC as a group has not yet contracted for services.[5]

Selection Issues:
the Rationale for Treating the Music Collection

Northwestern is now one of several libraries with an operational mass deacidification program, and to our knowledge the first to treat a music collection. University libraries with operational programs include Harvard and Johns Hopkins. Library administrators at Northwestern based their decision to treat the music collection on the following considerations:

- the Music Library is among the collections of distinction at Northwestern, known internationally for holdings of music composed since 1945;
- music has enduring value in the original format;
- operational ease–the music collection would require relatively little pre-treatment selection and evaluation.[6]

Music lends itself well to DEZ treatment because there are relatively few instances of coated paper or certain binding materials that are susceptible to inconsistent treatment results. Essentially, only those volumes that are already brittle or printed on acid-free paper would need to be pulled from a batch slated for DEZ treatment. The physical selection process is relatively simple and efficient.

The brittle volumes are evaluated for replacement by the Head of the Music Library. The preservation program thereby supports collection management functions, as the unneeded brittle volumes are weeded and the needed ones replaced.

Bibliographic Control

Prior to shipment to the Akzo deacidification plant, each volume is "charged-out" by Music Library student assistants to a deacidification patron record in NOTIS. For volumes with NOTIS catalog records, this procedure will generate a message in the public mode of the catalog record, "Out of building for deacidification. You may place a recall."

Although the entire music collection has been barcoded, about thirty-three percent is not yet cataloged online. Volumes are shipped for deacidification in shelf order, so this call number sequence can serve as a quick means to identify volumes without online records that are away for treatment.

The USMARC 583 field in the local bibliographic record is used to format preservation treatment information. Data elements include "deacidified," "Akzo," and the date of shipment. Since this data tends to be the same for each item in a shipment, a short code representing the standard data is input by student assistants, and the code later run through a translation table in a batch job to generate the terms. The 583 field data appears only in the staff mode of the local catalog.

Items not yet cataloged online are given priority in a concurrent retrospective conversion project. In the meantime, the date of shipment is noted by color-coded slips that are clipped to shelf list cards. Keeping track of the shipment date will allow for future preservation study on a shipment basis.

The DEZ Treatment Process

The library's Preservation Department is responsible for packing the volumes into wire crates following certain procedures to help ensure that the DEZ vapors will penetrate each closed volume. The wire crates are then put into a large insulated container called an overpack for shipment to the Akzo plant in Deer Park, Texas (near Houston).

At the Akzo plant, the wire crates are removed from the overpack and put directly into the treatment chamber; the volumes are not removed from the wire crates. The DEZ treatment process requires low pressure and a reduced paper moisture content, so air is pumped out of the chamber. The effect of the vacuum and a slight heating reduces the 5 to 6 percent of water normally present in paper. The amount of water removed is monitored indirectly by measuring the temperature of the volumes.[7]

When the desired conditions are reached, DEZ vapor is introduced to the treatment chamber. DEZ completely neutralizes all of the existing acid in the paper and also reacts with residual moisture in the paper to form a zinc oxide reserve. This alkaline buffer is evenly distributed throughout the paper and serves to neutralize any future acid formation.[8]

After the DEZ permeation is completed, the volumes are exposed to water vapor to recover a normal moisture content. This re-hydration phase takes about thirty hours. The entire deacidification cycle takes sixty hours.[9]

Quality Assurance

When the overpack arrives back at Northwestern, staff in the Preservation Department unpack the crates and thoroughly inspect each volume for any visible damage that may have been caused from the treatment process. A ten percent random sample from each shipment is sent to the library Conservation Lab for testing. The sample is checked for pH with a pH pen and for uniformity of treatment using a low-wave UV light. In addition, five sheets of paper are included with each shipment for post-treatment destructive testing. This paper is made into a slurry to test for alkaline reserve using a pH probe.

Rather than a statistically valid testing sample based on ongoing results, the Preservation Department currently believes that a ten percent random sample is a reasonable alternative given the visual inspection of each volume and the paper slurry testing. Records are kept for each part of the testing process.

DEZ treatment can cause commercial buckram bindings to blister. It can also weaken the adhesive of SE-LIN labels. These problems and subsequent repair expenses were anticipated from the test runs and the reports of other libraries. In the case of the music collection, about ten percent of the all the volumes receiving treatment have buckram bindings that must be rebound, and about ten percent of the treated volumes must be relabelled.

Many volumes come back from treatment with a slight odor that dissipates rapidly. Some staff members find it unpleasant. Tests by independent agencies indicate that the DEZ treatment residue is non-toxic.[10]

Before being returned to the stacks, the deacidified volumes and the volumes printed on acid-free paper are stamped on the spine with a gold infinity symbol, so that in the future any volumes that have not been deacidified will be immediately visible as a simple matter of shelf-reading.

Treatment Costs, Quantities, and Timetables

The cost of the chemical treatment is per overpack, regardless of the number of volumes it contains. Since the music is sent for packing in shelf order, the number of volumes per overpack varies considerably. One early shipment of only miniature scores contained over 1700 volumes. This bounty in volume numbers has been countered to some extent by shipments that include volumes larger than octavo. In the first year of the program, a total of about

5700 volumes have been treated in eight shipments. To date, the chemical treatment cost per volume is about $7.

The average time required to prepare a shipment is three weeks. The turn-around time for transport and treatment at the Akzo plant is five weeks. Quality control testing and other post-treatment processing at Northwestern take an additional three to four weeks. In sum, music being treated is off the shelves for about three months.

Conclusions

After one year of DEZ treatment operations, our experience at Northwestern demonstrates that mass deacidification is a feasible preservation option. The technical results of the program conform with the CIC task force test runs and the reports from other libraries. The program has now been expanded to another collection of distinction at Northwestern, the Africana Collection.

The occasional problem of the volume that must be re-labelled or rebound is not significant in relation to the overall benefits of the treatment. The most serious drawback of the program has involved public service considerations arising from the treatment of a circulating collection. Music Library patrons have had to contend with a three month absence of entire call number sequences (e.g., all of the organ sonatas). However, we believe that the long-term benefits of collection preservation outweigh the temporary problem.

The development of the DEZ process by Akzo and the Library of Congress has involved nearly twenty years of research and testing to resolve concerns regarding its efficacy and safety.[11] Further significant development or cost reduction of mass deacidification may be contingent on an increased level of library commitment to the currently available technologies.

Notes and References

1. For a brief account of the early development of the DEZ treatment process, see *Making Today's Books Last: Vapor-phase Deacidification at the Library of Congress* (Washington, D.C.: Library of Congress, 1985).

2. Robert Milevski, "Technical Aspects of Mass Deacidification," in *Proceedings of the New York State Seminar on Mass Deacidification* (New York: Columbia University Libraries, 1993), pp. 10–11.

3. Ibid., 10.

4. Richard Frieder, "CIC Cooperative Project–Logistics and Management Issues," in *Proceedings of the New York State Seminar on Mass Deacidification* (New York: Columbia University Libraries, 1993), pp. 51–61.

5. Ibid.

6. Eugene L. Wiemers, Jr., "Administrative and Selection Issues in Mass Deacidification," in *Proceedings of the New York State Seminar on Mass Deacidification* (New York: Columbia University Libraries, 1993), pp. 73–74.

7. Milevski, 10–11.

8. Ibid.

9. Ibid.

10. Ibid., 12–15.

11. James Stroud, "The Harry Ransom Humanities Research Center Diethyl Zinc Mass Deacidification Project," in *Proceedings of the New York State Seminar on Mass Deacidification* (New York: Columbia University Libraries, 1993), p. 36.

Preservation of Moving Images and Sound Recordings in the Music Library

Gerald Gibson

ABSTRACT: Sound and moving image media have been part of library and archival collections only for the briefest period of time. This means that the cumulative knowledge and experience that we have with such materials is modest when compared to that of more traditional paper and book materials. The success or failure of basic actions—cleaning, packaging, environment, playing, handling—is based in large part upon distinguishing the type (i.e., CD vs. grooved disc, or nitrate vs. safety-based film) of recording and the material or combination of materials of which it is made. The basic materials used for the manufacture of most audio and moving-image recordings are particularly dependent upon built-in degradation. A major concern in the conservation of all media is the environment in which they are stored: temperature, relative humidity, light, and cleanliness. We must rerecord some materials to ensure that their information will last. We must search to find more permanent storage media and to accept an archival format good for 50 or more years.

A brief review of moving images and sound recordings in the library is quite informative:

- The earliest audio recordings date from the late 1870s or the very early 1880s;
- Most CDs have been in library holdings barely five years;
- motion picture film, just now approaching its centenary, is less and less in most of our holdings;
- video recordings (excluding motion picture film) is just 25 years of age, being introduced by Ampex at the NAB show in April 1956.

Gerald Gibson is Head, Curatorial Section, Motion Picture, Broadcasting, and Recorded Sound Division, Library of Congress, Washington, DC.

With major exceptions, these media have been accepted as library and archival collections only for the briefest period of time. This means that the cumulative knowledge and experience that we have with such materials is modest when compared to that of more traditional paper and book materials. Nonetheless, over 1/3 of the 600,000 registrations submitted for U.S. Copyright registration in 1989 were either audio, film or video, and the rate is continuing to increase, as is the amount of such materials in libraries and archives throughout the world. In spite of this very short lifespan, there are well over a dozen different motion picture film formats, several dozens of audio carriers, and literally, hundreds of video carriers, each of which requires significantly different equipment to retrieve the data that they carry.

My coverage here will be limited to only the most common of those audio and moving-image carriers most frequently encountered in the modern working collection—disc, tape recordings, and motion picture film—and to the greatest dangers that I believe they face.

Basic Actions

The success or failure of basic actions—cleaning, packaging, environment, playing, handling—is based in large part upon distinguishing the type (i.e., CD vs. grooved disc, or nitrate vs. safety-based film) of recording and the material or combination of materials of which it is made. For example, a CD is safely cleaned by wiping it in a spoke fashion from the center, i.e., across the "grooves", while grooved discs must be cleaned by wiping in a circular or spiral direction, i.e., *not* across the grooves. It is equally important to know that various chemicals that may be helpful in safely cleaning a vinyl disc will destroy shellac, and may have harmful side effects for optical media. Similar problems exist with virtually all aspects of recording formats. The initial problem that one encounters, therefore, is distinguishing among similar formats, and recognizing the various materials of which they are and have been made.

MATERIALS

Commonly available disc recordings, whether carrying audio or moving-images, may vary in size from approximately 1-inch to 23-inches or more in diameter, and from 1/64 of an inch or less to 1/4 of an inch or more in thickness. They have been made of many of the substances known to us—whether as solid objects or as laminates—from wax and wood pulp to exotic, rare, and costly metals. They can be very stable and chemically inert or highly combustible and potentially harmful to things around them.

The signal on a disc may be analog or digital, recorded acoustically, electrically or optically, using either a lateral or a vertical cutting head and playback stylus or a laser, produced by cutting, embossing, magnetizing, and photographic engraving processes. The artifact so produced may be a totally unique item that never leaves the confines of the area in which it is made, or it may be part of a commercial mass production in the millions of copies with world wide distribution. Discs can play at speeds of less than ten to greater than 500 revolutions per minute (rpm). Their styli- —when they have one—may have a tip radius varying from .5 to 35 mils, with intended tracking weights of less than 1/4 of a gram to several or more pounds.

Grooved discs—Selectavision video, LPs, 45s, et al.—generally are made of various plastics and plastic compounds. Optical discs, audio and moving-image alike, are laminates of plastics or glass and various metal foils, with sundry lacquers used to seal the package. In archives and some notable libraries, 78s and acetate discs are also commonly found. 78s were, most generally, made of shellac and shellac compounds, although there were a notable number made of plastics, rubber, cellulose, and various laminate combinations. Acetate discs are laminates with a base of metal, wood products or glass, with a coating of either ethyl cellulose, cellulose acetate, or nitrocellulose.

Magnetic recordings have been made in several different forms, notably tape and disc. They have been made of solid metal bands and discs, as well as paper and various cellulose and polyester discs. These are coated with a wide variety of materials that can take and hold a magnetic charge. The number of different videotape formats—a recording medium just 35 years old—is now over 300, meaning that if a given collection is going to colntain all available media it would have to have a veritible Noah's Ark of equipment.

Though the simplest to use of the moving-image carriers, as well as probably the most stable with the highest quality image, motion picture film is the most expensive to acquire, to store and to use. For example, a one hour color movie can require up to seven reels of project print, plus another twenty-eight reels of materials, and can cost in excess of $50,000, requiring substantial space for storage. A comparable video copy and master would occupy one cassette and one reel of tape, cost less than $500 and require relatively little space for storage.

Controlling Degradation

Once the initial problem of recognition of materials is resolved, the principal problems of preservation can be considered. As Pickett and Lemcoe pointed out some 30 years ago, the resistance of an article to degradation is built into it at the time of manufacture.[1] The basic materials used for the manufacture of most audio and moving-image recordings are particularly dependent upon this fact. None of the widely held media were designed for long-term storage, but rather for playback qualities and low cost manufacture. What follows then are some of the principal steps that we can take to control the factors contributing to the acceleration of degradation so that recordings can last for the life-span that was built into them.

The principal problems encountered with this medium are warpage, heavy wear, breakage, damaged edges, delamination and micro-biological deterioration. In mass produced grooved discs the single greatest problem is groove wear. For tape recordings, for some mass produced discs, and for all motion picture film the greatest danger is delamination, or separation of the surface carrying the data from its core or backing, with print through being a significant concern for magnetic tape. Delamination and corrosion of the metallic reflective surface seem to be the two principal problems for optical disc media.

In general, problems of warpage, breakage, broken and crinkled edges and micro-biological deterioration are controllable by careful handling, cleaning, packaging and storage.

Groove wear can be reduced significantly by proper maintenance of the playback equipment, including regular inspection of the weight, tracking and conditions of the stylus, use of the proper stylus for the groove and regular cleaning of the item both before playing or storage.

Prevention and control of delamination and of corrosion of optical reflective surfaces are far more difficult, since they usually have already begun before we are aware there is an active danger. Plus, they are frequently a problem of poor quality control in the manufacturing of the carrier. The principal steps that can be taken to slow this process are careful handling and cleaning, and proper maintenance of the storage conditions: packaging, environment, and physical arrangement on the shelf. From all reports the two most important factors are the relative humidity and the temperature.

Of particular interest to all of us concerned with preservation of such media is the latest film horror, called *vinegar syndrome*. First discussed within the last five or six years, we are now learning that there is a real problem facing us with any cellulose based materials, whether nitrate, diacetate, or triacetate. It appears that these materials, used in many different ways in our collections, are returning to their original chemical components. The odor of acidic acid, or vinegar, is most noticeable in areas with moderate to poor air circulation where quantities of safety motion picture film are stored. The film quickly shows a number of stages of deterioration: first the strong vinegar smell, then rusting or discoloration of the container, then visual breakdown of the film, and finally the film becomes so brittle that it is unusable, it cannot be put through a projector or printer, the emulsion separates from its carrier base, and the film is totally useless. As bad as this may seem, it seems that the gasses given off in the process act as an air-borne contaminant that spreads the problem to film that has not yet shown any symptoms. Also frightening is the supposition that all cellulose materials are susceptible to this problem, including microfilm and acetate discs. There is, as yet, no know treatment. The suggestion that has recently come from the Rochester Institute of Technology's IPI is that all materials susceptible to the problem should be stored in controlled environments with a steady temperature below 40° and 30% R/H, with a staged copying of the most important items.

There are a number of products on the market that claim to reduce surface wear and to cut down on the static electricity on the surface of the recording, thus lessening dust attraction. Other products available are designed to aid in removing the build up of dirt and dust prior to playing. There are great reservations about applying such products to recordings because it is not known what the long term effect will be. Thus, with the exception of specific applications for cleaning given below, the use of such treatments is not recommended. Only in the most extreme cases should they be used for anything other than controlled testing, or until there is clear information that they do no unnecessary harm.

A problem in conservation of disc recordings is the presence of a label affixed, printed or embossed directly onto its surface. A label, with glue or heat seals, inks and dyes, introduces a new set of problems to disc preservation, e.g., dissolution in the cleaning or aging process, fading in the general aging process, and negative acidic effects on the disc.[2] Experience has shown that parts of the label might dissolve, but they can be protected with care in the cleaning and handling process. The label is, generally, of a fairly high quality, is reasonably low in acidity, and is resistant to molds.

The question of CDs being destroyed by inks used on their labels first came to public attention in 1988. The report in the *Manchester Guardian* concluded that the inks used in printing labels on CDs were eating through the seal of the CD, allowing the foil that holds the encoded data to corrode, thus destroying the recordings.[3] Representatives of Sony and Phillips responded that where adequate quality control is exerted during the manufacturing process, no problem exists.

As with most things in this field, we are certain of very little regarding cleaning. What we know is based generally upon trial and error, not upon controlled, scientific study. For example, I favor certain procedures because they have worked well for me, personally and because they do not *appear* to harm the item. Only time will confirm these conclusions.

One thing is certain: playing a dirty recording, regardless of its format, is one of the most damaging things you can do to it. Dirt is ground into its surface, where it creates abrasions and unwanted variations in the playing surface. These, in turn, cause distortion in the transmitted signal, complicate and exaggerate the aging process, and, in extreme cases, actually obliterate the signal and prevent its being read.

Nor should one assume that new recordings are clean. Almost certainly they are not. The only proof one needs for this is to wipe the surface of a new cording with a soft, clean white cloth. Any item that is to be played should be cleaned first. Likewise, any item to be stored should be cleaned prior to packaging and storage. Otherwise, enough damage can be done to prevent future retrieval of an acceptable signal.

There are several successful methods for cleaning recordings. The mechanical techniques available include ultrasonics, vacuum machines, and, for buffing, of course, there is always cleaning by hand. The custom built ultrasonic machines for cleaning discs are at the Swedish Radio, the National Archives of Canada and the Library of Congress. I have not seen an ultrasonic machine for cleaning tapes.

More common for disc formats is the vacuum type machine. The disc is secured on the cleaning machines's turntable, cleaning liquid is applied through a cleaning brush, the solution is worked into the grooves of the disc by the brush by rotating the turntable, and the liquid and the debris it has loosened are removed by a vacuum device built into the machine. Vacuum type machines for discs are manufactured by a number of firms, such as Keith Monks, Nitty Gritty and VPI. All work well to very well, but the VPI give among the best service while maintaining an excellent maintenance record for the money. The laser disc cleaners, also work quite well, with the disc secured to the turntable, a buffing solution applied by hand, and the disc moved back and forth in a stroking motion and buffed by a pad built into the lid of the machine.

The buffing cleaners for tape used in most archival collections and professional recording studios of which I am aware places a roll of a lint-free paper material—called *pellon*—on a roller moving in the opposite direction to the tape to be cleaned. As the tape is wound onto its take-up reel it moves against the *pellon* and is wiped or buffed by it.

If the only means available for cleaning is by hand, by all means do so, but carefully. When hand cleaning, most recordings should be cleaned by gently wiping them with a clean, soft, lint free cotton velvet cloth or cleaning brush, moistened with the cleaning agent. The cleaning is done in a circular motion *with* the grooves for grooved discs, in a spoke or radial direction, going *across* the "grooves" for laser discs, and for the length of the tape or film.

The type of cleaning solution to use depends upon the recording to be cleaned, the materials of which it is made, and the dirt and debris to be cleansed from its surface. Whether it is a solid or a laminated object must also be taken into consideration. Except in emergency situations, avoid cleaning fluids containing alcohol. Also, because of the wide variety of materials used in their manufacturer and to the possibility of breakdown of the bond between their surface and base, alcohol should not be used to clean laminated recordings, disc, tape and cylinder alike.

At the Library of Congress we use Freon TF for really dirty items, for most tape materials, and for most acetate materials. The Library uses a solution such as the DiscWasher D-4+ for vinyl records and D-4+ Shellac Formula for shellac recordings in a 4 to 1 solution with distilled water. This cleaner is used whether the recording is being cleaned by vacuum machine or by hand. Alcohol is used only in extreme cases, with "normal" cleaning following. Extreme care must be used on applications of any liquid to laminated recordings—disc, tape or film—particularly those with a wood or paper base, for the base will expand if it gets wet, causing the recording surface to warp and break even faster than normal.

Routine cleaning of equipment—such as stylus and tape heads—*must* accompany any record cleaning procedure. The best way that we have found to clean a stylus is using a specially designed stylus cleaning brush with short, tightly packed bristles, such as those from DiscWasher or LAST. Another acceptable method is to use an ultrasonic stylus cleaner, such as those from Signet or Hervic. The manufacturers of such ultrasonic devices recommend that they be used in conjunction with cleaning fluids that they furnish. I am not aware of a) any reported problems with this procedure or b) independent analysis to determine if there is reason not to follow these recommendations. Tape heads are cleaned by hand, using Q-tips and either freon TF or alcohol. Demagnetizing of the heads is carried out at the same time.

Once a recording has been cleaned, it should *not* be put into the same dirty container from which it was taken. If you must keep the container because of historical or content information, clean it carefully and use an inner sleeve or liner with it. Paper inner sleeves should be avoided because the paper breaks down over time and contaminates the surface and grooves of the recording with paper debris. An inner liner chemically similar or identical with the item should be avoided as like items, particularly plastics, tend to adhere to one another. According to some reports, materials similar in composition allow stabilizers or plasticizer to migrate between the items. Thus, poly*vinyl* sleeves should not be used because they are too like the polyvinyl of LP records. Instead, use an inner sleeve made of or lined with high density poly*ethylene* or poly*urethane*, as are available from such firms as DiscWasher, V.R.P., and Mobile Fidelity. For disc storage where the original jacket is not retained, I recommend a sleeve of polyethylene-foil-paper board based on Pickett & Lemcoe's recommendations.[4] A good disc package, developed by the Library of Congress from the principles proposed by Pickett and Lemcoe, is available from Shield Pack, Inc., of Monroe, LA, the only known source for the container.

For many years the only option available for packaging tape recordings was the container in which they came. As an outgrowth of another problem dealing with availability of containers for film the National Archives and the Library of Congress asked the National Bureau of Standards for suggestions on the chemical make-up of containers for magnetic tape. Their response was for a chemically inert material that could be shaped into the desired package—polypropylene plastic with fire retardant. Carbon black or titanium dioxide are the acceptable coloring agents. The container, manufactured by the Plastic Reel Corp. of America (PRC), has a UL fire rating of V-2 (reasonably good, and much better than almost all other plastics that go into our various collections), is very strong (it holds my 200 pound weight without being crushed or breaking), and has many of the design features that Pickett and Lemcoe recommend.[5]

An improved design of this tape box, just introduced by 3M, has just been adopted by the Library of Congress for its collection. Even with these improvements in design, not all of the Pickett and Lemcoe suggestions for such a container have been realized. Capability to do this is available with a package, initially designed for film and part of a staging/packaging procedure developed by the Swedish Film Institute. This process calls for the film to be properly cleaned and wound, staged in an environmental chamber until it reaches the desired R/H and then vacuum sealed into a poly/foil bag. LC now purchases its bags from Shield Pack, Inc. Although we have not yet experimented with the process, it seems reasonable to presume that the same system would be applicable to magnetic tape.

Environment

One of the major concerns in the conservation of all media is the environment in which they are stored: temperature, relative humidity, light, and cleanliness. Sound and moving-image media are no exception. Two basic facts should be remembered when considering the storage environment: an item will generally double its predicted life span for every 10°C the storage temperature can be lowered; for the growth of the majority of mildews the optimum environment is 79–82°F and 70+% relative humidity. The recommendations Pickett and Lemcoe made in the 1950s are still accepted: 70°F, 50% relative humidity.[6] New information regarding environment for archival audio/visual media has lowered the desired relative humidity to 35%, ± 5%, with tape storage aiming at an even lower reading of 20%. The present recommendation for long term, archival storage calls for the temperature to be as cool as possible, but above freezing, going well beyond the Pickett and Lemcoe suggested 50°F. All agree that stability is essential, and that any significant cycling of either the temperature or the relative humidity, much less both, will cause major problems in the future.

Where at all possible, store all recordings in a darkened room, but always away from sunlight and from artificial lighting of the shorter wave lengths.

The actual shelving units used should allow discs and tapes to stand vertically, and—by present thinking—for film to be flat. Dividers hould support the disc and tape packages from top to bottom, and from front to back, attached in such a way as to be sure that they will not slip accidentally, and placed at regular intervals of not more than 5-inches for discs, and ten-inches for standard audio tapes. Units must be sufficiently strong to support the fairly substantial weight (the proper packaged LP records required fully to load a 36" × 70" shelf unit will weigh over 500 pounds; and equal quantity (c.180) of 1,200' cans of 16mm film will weigh almost the same).

The realm of the laser disc is still so new that we are only beginning to understand their problems. Nonetheless, several generalities can be made: they should be stored in the same vertical position as any other disc; they appear (independent testing has not yet been carried out) to respond favorably to the same temperature, humidity, and environmental conditions as other discs; their surfaces need to be protected from dirt, scratches, and abrasions, and care should be taken in handling them.

As with all new media, there are still a number of questions to answer and problems to resolve with the optical disc. Among them are what is the potential life of the package; how important are fluctuations in heat and humidity to their long term stability and successful data retrieval; is light of particular wave lengths a significant factor in deterioration, and if so, are they the same U/V wave lengths that we wish to avoid with other plastics; will the clear surface scratch easily or discolor with age, or because of heat, humidity, and/or light; will any of the various components of the package-plastics, inks, various metals interact to breakdown the package and/or shorten anticipated life; under what conditions will the laminated disc separate?

A number of very real problems have begun to surface with laser discs. Among them is "Laser Rot" (a situation where the image begins in good condition, and then, over time, deteriorates into what has been described as "technicolor confetti;" delamination of the various strata of the disc; and deterioration or destruction of the pits that carry the data, reportedly because the seal of the discs is penetrated by acids in the ink used to print these. These phenomena are, thus far, only rarely encountered (I saw my very first delaminated CD during a visit to Vienna this past September; and my first example of "Laser Rot" just last week). The industry reports that all such laser disc problems are caused by poor quality control during the manufacturing process and not to flaws in the design or its various component parts.

One thing to keep in mind is that equipment to make instantaneous digital recordings is not yet standardized. The Association for Recorded Sound Collections' Associated Audio Archives Committee has taken the position that:[7]

72 PRESERVATION OF MOVING IMAGES

> The combination of digital . . . recorders, magnetic recorders using magnetic tape, and digital formats is not appropriate for the generation *of archival preservation transfer copies* of . . . recordings at this time [March 1987] for the following reasons:
> 1. there are no nationally accepted standards for the various digital records and formats;
> 2. the . . . industry has yet to resolve its conflicting systems; [and]
> 3. neither equipment nor formats have yet been tested or proven reliable in an archival setting for making archival preservation transfer copies.

The same position has been adopted by others, including the IASA and AES.

When the industry and the various national and international standardization bodies do come to agreement, particularly so for the instantaneous write-once disc, presuming the shelf life is reasonably acceptable, I believe that digital recording will become the preferred archival rerecording and storage standard. Until that time I agree with and support the ARSC/AAA position: as librarians and archivists we must take a wait and see attitude for digital signals for archival storage.

Conclusion

As I presented at the beginning of this paper, one of the major problems that must be faced when dealing with these media is the wide variety of forms, and the even wider variety of materials of which they are made. As technology continues to evolve we find that an even greater problem is the speed with which formats, materials, and equipment become obsolete. Thus, an archival collection finds itself needing to acquire and stock not only the carriers of the information we seek and the equipment that will allow us to "read" the information, but the spare parts and the mechanical expertise to keep the equipment in working order. Some suggest that the solution is to re-record all recordings onto whatever is the standard of the day. This is totally unfeasible, if for cost alone. To take one example: if the Library of Congress were faced with rerecording each of the 80,000+ audio items it received in the last 12 months, alone, the cost would be well over $6,000,000 just for blank tape and engineers time. If it were to undertake the rerecording of its entire audio collection the cost would be an estimated $200,000,000, in 1991 dollars. Further, at the rate format and equipment change, another rerecording of each of these items could be anticipated within the next 10 to 20 years. Additional expenses must include space to house the "new" copies, staff to handle and maintain the collection, and adequate environment to store them in a manner that will ensure their physical existence until that next rerecording took place. Finally, there is the single most costly thing that our collections face: catalog control.

Obviously we must rerecord some materials to ensure that their information will last. To undertake such a costly action because the industry wants to bring a new technology onto the market, especially one for which they, themselves, have not yet adopted standards, seems foolish and extravagant. Further, it seems only reasonable that we as the preservers of our cultural heritage must realize the sizeable contribution we make to the profits of that industry and take an active stand for reason and rationale in what appears to be an ever increasing evolution of new technologies that offer minimal, if any, improvements in the preservation, conservation, organization, storage, or dissemination of our collective knowledge.

Clearly, the solution cannot be endlessly to rerecord holdings. We must search to find a more permanent storage media and to accept an archival format good for 50 or more years. Further, we must actively and aggressively work together, since the job is far to large for any one or two collections to undertake. We must carry out coordinated research into the various factors that affect the long term storage and retrieval of the data and materials in our collections. We must work together to build the shared pool of knowledge that is necessary to prevent premature failure of the items in our care, and, thus, loss of the knowledge of our civilization. Only in that manner can we assure that the information that they carry will be transmitted to future generations.

References

1. Pickett, A.G., and M.M. Lemcoe, *Preservation And Storage Of Sound Recordings ; A Study supported by a grant from the Rockefeller Foundation* (Washington, DC: Library of Congress, 1959), p. 5.
2. Erlichman, James. "Compact Discs' Fade Out After Eight Years' Use" *Guardian* (June 29, 1988) p. 1.
3. Ibid.
4. Pickett, A.G., and M.M. Lemcoe, *Preservation*, p. 48.
5. Ibid., p. 61.
6. Ibid., p. 45.
7. Association for Recorded Sound Collections. Associated Audio Archives Committee. *Audio preservation: A Planning Study* (Silver Spring, MD: Association for Recorded Sound Collections, 1987).

Appendix A: Selected Bibliography

SOUND RECORDINGS

Alten, Stanley R. *Audio in media*, 2nd ed. Belmont, California: Wadsworth Pub. Co., 1986.

Association for Recorded Sound Collections. Associated Audio Archives Committee. *Audio Preservation: a planning study*. Silver Spring Maryland: Association for Recorded Sound Collections, 1987.

Borwick, John, editor. *Sound recording practice*, 2nd ed. London: Oxford University Press, 1980.

Brock-Nannestad, George. "A Comment and Further Recommendations International Rerecording Standards" *ARSC Journal* Vol. 19:2–3, 1987.

Doesburg Carl L. "Costs of Storage in Sound Archives." *Phonographic Bulletin* No. 54 (July 1989).

Fox, Barry. "Tests prove CD's can self destruct." *New Scientist* 7 (July 1988).

Frow, George L. and Albert F. Sefl. *The Edison cylinder phonographs*. Sevenoaks, Kent, England: George L Frow, 1978.

Gibson, Gerald. "Decay and Degradation of Disc and Cylinder Recordings in Storage", in *Audio Preservation: a planning study*. Silver Spring, Maryland: Association for Recorded Sound Collections, 1987.

Harkness, Clifford. "Criteria for Air Conditioning in Audio-Visual Archives" in *Archiving the Audio-Visual Heritage*, Berlin: FIAF, 1988.

Lechleitner, Franz. "The Construction of Cylinder Replay Machines" in *Archiving the Audio-Visual Heritage*, Berlin: FIAF, 1988.

McWilliams, Jerry. *The Preservation and Restoration of Sound Recordings*. Nashville: American Association for State and Local History, 1979.

McWilliams, Jerry. "Storage, Care, and Preservation of Sound Recordings-a Bibliography.," *ARSC Journal 9:2* (1977).

Pickett, A.G. and M.M. Lemcoe. *Preservation and storage of sound recordings*. Washington, D.C.: Library of Congress, 1959.

Read, Oliver. *The recording and reproduction of sound*, 2nd ed. Indianapolis: H.W. Sams, 1952.

Read, Oliver, and Walter L. Welch. *From Tin Foil to Stereo: Evolution of the Phonograph*, rev. and enl. 2nd ed. Indianapolis: H.W. Sams, 1976.

Schuller, Dietrich. "Preliminary recommendations for fire precautions and fire extinguishing methods in sound archives." *Phonographic Bulletin*, 35 (March 1983).

Schuller, Dietrich. "The Costs of Storage and Preservation." *Phonographic Bulletin* No. 54 (July 1989).

Storm, William D. "The Implementation of Proposed Standards for Copying Audio Recordings" in *Archiving the Audio-Visual Heritage* Berlin: FIAF, 1988.

Welch, Walter L. "Preservation and Restoration of Authenticity in Sound Recordings." *Library Trends* 21 (July 1972).

Wile, Raymond R. Etching the Human Voice: The Berliner invention of the Gramophone. *ARSC Journal 21:1* (Spring 1990).

Wile, Raymond R. "The Edison Invention of the Phonograph." *ARSC Journal,* Vol 14:2, 1982.

MAGNETIC MEDIA

Association for Recorded Sound Collections. Associated Audio Archives Committee. *Audio Preservation: A Planning Study.* Silver Spring, Maryland: Association for Recorded Sound Collections, 1987.

Bertram, Neal and Michael K. Stafford. "The Print-Through Phenomena." *Journal of the Audio Engineering Society* 28:10 (October 1980).

Bertram, H.N., and A. Eshel. *Recording Media Archival Attributes-* (Magnetic). Redwood City,CA: Ampex Corporation, 1979.

Bertram, H.N., and E.F. Cuddihy. "Kinetics of the Humid Aging of Magnetic Recording Tape." *Institute of Electrical and Electronics Engineers (IEEE) Transactions on Magnetics* 18: 5 (September 1982).

Bradshaw, R., et. al. "Chemical and Mechanical Performance of Flexible Magnetic Tape Containing Chromium Dioxide." *I.B.M. Journal of Research and Development* 30:2 (March 1986).

Brown, D.W., R.E. Lowery and L.E. Smith. *Predictions of Long-Term Stability of Polyester-Based Recording Media.* National Bureau of Standards Institute Report 86-3474. Progress report to June 1986. Washington, D.C.: National Bureau of Standards, 1986.

Calmes, Alan. "New Preservation Concern: Video Recordings": *Commission on Preservation and Access Newsletter, 22* (April 1990) Washington: Commission on Preservation and Access, 1990.

Camras, Marvin. *Magnetic RecordingHandbook.* New York: Van Nostrand Reinhold Company, 1988.

Committee on Preservation of Historical Records. *Preservation of Historical Records: Magnetic Recording Media.* Washington, D.C.: National Academy Press, 1986. Cuddihy, Edward F. "Aging of Magnetic Recording Tape." *IEEE Transactions on Marnetics* 16:4 (July 1980).

―――"Magnetic Recording Tape; A Discussion of the Material Properties of Tape Having Relevance to the Storage, Performance, and System Effects." *Communication.*, 1982.

―――"Hygroscopic Properties of Magnetic Recording Tape." *IEEE Transactions on Magneticsl* 12:2 (March 1976).

Davison, P.S., P. Giles and D.A.R. Matthews. "Aging of Magnetic Tape: A Critical Bibliography and Comparison of Literature Sources." *The Computer Journal* 11: 241-246.

Fontaine, L.M. Degradation de l'Enregistrement Magnetique Audio; *Processus de Deterioration de l'Enregistrement Analogique.* 1987 (unpublished).

Geller, S.B. *Care and Handling of Computer Magnetic Storage Media.* NBS Special Publication 500-101. Washington, D.C.: Institute for Computer Sciences and Technology, National Bureau of Standards, 1983.

Hendriks, Klaus. "The Stability and Preservation of Recorded Images." *Image Processes and Materials* New York: Van Nostrand Reinhold, 1989.

Kalil, Ford, ed. *Magnetic Tape Recordineg for the Eighties.* NASA Reference Publication 1075. Tape Head Interface Committee, 1982.

Mallinson, J.C. "The Next Decade in Magnetic Recording." *IEEE Transactions on Magnetics* 21:3 (May 1985).

—— "On the Preservation of Human and Machine Readable Records." *International Technology and Libraries.* (March 1988).

Olson, Nancy B. "Hanging Your Software Up to Dry." *College and Research Libraries News* 47:10 (November 1986).

Parson, Douglas "Videotape Conservation and Restoration: Usual Defects, Possible Remedies," *Minutes and Working Papers of the FIAT/IFTA 6th General Assembly,* 29th September–1st October, 1986, Montreal. Madrid: International Federation of TV Archives (FIAT/IFTA), 1987.

Rikiake, Tsuneji. *Magnetic and Electromagnetic Shielding.* Tokyo; Terra Scientific Pub. Co.; Dordrecht; Boston: D. Reidel Pub. Co,; Hingham, Massachusetts, U.S.A., 1987. Sold and distributed in the U.S.A. and Canada by Kluwer Academic Publishers.

Pickett, A.G., and M.M. Lemcoe. *Preservation and Storage of Sound Recordings.* Washington, D.C.: Library of Congress, 1959.

"Practice Safe Computing." in *Special List, The Newsletter of Special Libraries Association,* Vol. 13 (No. 7) July 1990.

Richmond, Joseph C. *Transfer of Monochrome Video Information from Magnetic Tape to Motion Picture Film for Archival Storage.* Washington, D.C.: US. Department of Commerce, National Bureau of Standards, 1978.

Smolian, Steven. "Preservation, Deterioration and Restoration of Recording Tape." *ARSC Journal* Vol. 19:2–3, 1987.

Sound Tape Recording, Television Tape Recording, and Film Techniques for the International Exchange of Programmes. Geneva: International Telecoommunication Union, International Radop Consulative Committee, 1985.

APPENDIX A

Welz, Gehard. "On the Problem of Storing Videotapes" *Archiving the Audio/Visual Heritage: a joint technical symposium.* Postprints of a joint technical symposium held in Berlin, Germany in 1988 and sponsored by FIAT, FIAF, IASA, and ICA.

Wheeler, Jim. "Increasing the Life of Your Audio Tape" *Journal of the Audio Engineering Society* Vol. 36:4 (April 1988).

——."Long-term Storage of Videotape" *SMPTE Journal* (June 1983).

Appendix B: Preservation Supplies for Sound Recordings

Disc cleaning

Discwasher
4310 Transworld Road
Schiller Park, IL 60176
1-800-325-0573

The LAST Factory
2015 Research Drive
Livermore, CA 94550
(415) 449-9449

Professional disc cleaning machines

Keith Monks Audio Laboratory
c/o Allied Broadcasting Equipment
3712 National Road West Richmond, IN 47374
(314) 962-8596

Nitty Gritty Record Care Products
4650 Arrow Highway #F4
Montclair, CA 91763
(714) 625-5525

VPI Industries, Inc.
77 Cliffwood Ave. #3B
Cliffwood, NJ 07721
(201) 946-8578

Jackets, reels, boxes, and containers

Shield Pack, Inc.
2301 Downing Pines Road

West Monore, Louisiana 71291
(318) 387-4743

3M
3M Center Building, 223-5N-01
St. Paul, MN 55144-1000
1 (800) 551-5185

University Products
517 Main Street
P.O. Box 101
Holyoak, MA 01041
1 (800) 628-1912

Conservation Resources International
8000 H Forbes Place
Springfield, VA 22151 (USA)
1-800-6%-6932

Plastic Reel Corporation of America
Brisbin Avenue
Lyndhurst, NJ 07071
(201) 933-5100

Audio "78" Archival Supplies
P.O. Box 387
1010 Grand Teton
Pacifica, CA 94044
(415) 359-7431

Record jacket inner sleeves

Angstrom db
210 S. 8th Street
Lewiston, NY 14092
(800) 378-8193
Specify Nagaoka

Audio Mobile
2573 Shattuck Avenue
Berkeley, CA 94704
(415) 548-8733
Specify high-density

Fidelity
1260 Holm Road
Petaluma, CA 94952
(800) 423-5759
Specify ,"Original
sleeve model 102 polypropylene sleeve Master' sleeve
($ 15.00/100) '

Discwasher
(address above)
Specify VRP sleeve

Stylus cleaners

(Ultrasonic)
Signet
4701 Hudson Drive
Stow, Ohio 44224 (USA)
(216) 668-9400

(Brush)
The Last Factory (address above)
Discwasher (address above)

Appendix C:
Audio Reformatting Fact Sheets

The Rodgers and Hammerstein Archives of Recorded Sound
New York Public Library, Performing Arts Research Center
New York, NY

Organization and Staffing

    The Rodgers and Hammerstein (R&H) Archives is one of four NYPL performing arts research collections located at Lincoln Center. The recording laboratory at R & H is staffed by four sound engineers who do audio reformatting. Note: Reformatting is often called audio transfer by audio engineers.

Scope of Activities

The types of material reformatted include:
- defunct or obsolete formats (i.e, acetate tapes and disks, and cylinders)
- High-use items (anything requested 10 times and reference materials)
- Live recordings and radio broadcasts
- Unique or artifactually valuable items

Equipment available

Basic equipment for reformatting sound recordings includes:
- TechnicSP 15 Turntable with a specially designed base for 16 inch transcription.
- SME Tone arm
- Stanton 5OOAL Cartridge
- OWL Stylus

-OWL Restoration Module for Playback Equalization
-Barclay Spectral Analyzer
-Keith Monks disk cleaning machine (using distilled water)
-Open reel tape machines

General Procedures

The head engineer is available for free consultation and for work on funded cooperativeprojects. Depending on the material to be preserved, a preservation copy and a service copy are produced and the original is retained, depending on its condition. Littleor no filtering is done, the goal is to duplicate the original faithfully; not to improve its quality. A computer system which uses the software package Advanced Revelation links the sound engineering studio and the cataloging unit.

Tape

AGFA468 open reel tape

Storage and Access

Master tapes are stored on open shelving within the laboratory. The building is climate controlled and there are no additional controls in the tape storage area. R & H is currently reevaluating storage conditions and practices and is considering housing master tapes and originals at separate off-site facilities. Cassette tape service copies are made for patron use upon request. In-house playback is provided at listening carrels that contain high-quality audio components.

APPENDIX C

The Belfer Audio Laboratory and Archive
Syracuse University, Syracuse, New York

Organization

Belfer is a functionally separate unit within the Syracuse University Library system. Its Director reports to the University Librarian.

Scope of Activities

Large quantities of preservation copies are made during grant-funded projects directed towards specific portions of the archive's holdings. Deteriorating items are also put onto tape on a case-by-case basis. These for the most part include cylinders and acetate tapes and discs. Materials requested for listening/study are put on master reels and then to cassette for research use at the library.

Equipment available

    4 2-track MCI tape decks
    2 4-track MCI tape decks
    1 MCI 16-track automated console
    1 Ramsa 16-track console
    2 Denon cassette decks
    2 Technics variable speed turntables
    2 QRK 16" turntables
    1 pair UREI time-aligned monitor speakers
    McIntosh power amplifiers
    Packburn Transient Noise Suppressors
    Packburn Continuous Noise Suppressors
    2 UREI 565 filter sets

2 UREI 527A Third Octave filters
1 BTX audio editing system
1 Crown BDP-2 Audio Microprocessor
1 B&K Dual Channel FFT Spectrum Analyzer
1 Nikon Optical Comparator
4 IBM Personal Computers
IBM Mainframe computer

Recording procedures

MONO recording—full-track @ 7.5 ips on 1/4" tape reel's. STEREO recording—2 track @ 7.5 ips. Most reels used are 10 1/2" in diameter. For preservation storage copies, no equalization or filtering is done. Processing may be done for service copies if deemed appropriate.

Tape

Scotch 808 1/4"—1200 ' Lo-Print (7" and 10 1/2" reels)
Scotch 226 1/2"—2500 ' Lo-Print (10 1/2" reels)
Scotch Cassettes—AVX Studio Master 20, 30, 46, and 60 minute lengths

Storage and Access

Master tapes are numbered and indexed on a PC program and shelved vertically. Cassette copies for listening are placed temporarily in the Library for use by students and other researchers (there are no listening carrels in the Belfer building). Cassette copies are also provided for researchers more than 100 miles from Syracuse if all copyright clearances have been obtained by the user in advance and in writing.

(5/91)

APPENDIX C

Historical Recordings Collection
General Libraries
University of Texas, Austin, TX

Organization and Staffing

All reformatting activities are carried out by staff in the Historical Recordings Collection in the Fine Arts Library.

Scope of Activities

Only information recorded on chemically unstable sound carriers (e.g., acetate-based recordings) is reformatted.

Equipment available

Reformatting and playback is done using equipment from various manufacturers including: Technics, Owl, Packburn, Orban, Shure, and Otari.

General Procedures

Insofar as it is possible to produce an "archival" sound recording, the staff of the Historical Recordings Collection follow a variety of technical standards and recommendations. Reformatting in particular is done following technical recommendations outlined in *Audio Preservation: A Planning Study* (1987).

Tape

AGFA professional quality, polyester-based, low print-through, reel-to-reel tape.

APPENDIX C 89

Storage and Access

Rare master recordings are stored upright on 10.5 inch, slotless-hub metal reels, tails out. Other master recordings are stored upright on 10.5 inch plastic reels. Cassette service copies are produced from master tapes.

The General Libraries practices an open access policy. Masters are used only to generate service copies; they are not accessible for patron use. Those submitting works to the Historical Recordings Collection regulate service copy distribution of their works through deposit agreements established at the time of deposit. Some collections may also have special restrictions placed on their use, which are also designated by the owner.

Index

Association for Library Collections & Technical Services, Preservation of Library Materials Section, Education Committee, 1
Association of College and Research Libraries, Rare Books and Manuscripts Section, 1
Association of Recorded Sound Collections, 10; Associated Audio Archives Committee, 33, 71–72
Akzo Chemicals (Firm), 52
Audio Engineering Society, Preservation Committee, 33

Beethoven, Ludwig van, 31
Bernstein, Leonard, 18
binderies, 26–29
binding, condition of, as variable in survey; 42–44; construction, as variable in survey, 42; origin of, as variable in survey, 41
Booklab, 20
Brahms, Johannes, 18
brass-bands, New Orleans, La., 2–3
brittle books, in Juilliard School survey, 37–38
Buchanan, Sara, 35–36

Calkins, Kenneth, 51–58
call number, as variable in survey, 39
Cloonan, Michele, 1
Coleman, Sandra, 35–36
Columbia University, Conservation Program, 15, 21–23
Commission on Preservation and Access, 21

Committee on Institutional Cooperation, 52
Cornell University, 21
country of publication, as variable in survey, 39–40
covers, condition of, as variable in survey, 42, 43
Cunningham, Ellen, 1

date, copyright, as variable in survey, 40; accession/cataloging, as variable in survey, 40
David, Ferdinand, 19
degradation, control of, 62–63
delamination, 63
diethyl zinc (DEZ), treatment process, 54–55; used for mass deacidification, 52
digital scanning, for preservation purposes, 21
Draper, Ruth (1884–1956), 18
Draper, Ruth Dana (1850–1914), 18

Eastman School of Music, 20
environmental considerations, for preservation, 24–26

Gibson, Gerald, 59–74
Gottlieb, Jane, 1–2, 12–34
groove wear, 63

Hanson, Martha, 1

International Association of Music Libraries, Archives, and Documentation Centres (IAML), 10

Juilliard School, Archives, 13; circulation system at, 37; collection

INDEX 91

management program, 14–17;condition survey, 2, 39–45; Library, 12–34; preservation projects, 17–23; special collections, 16

laser discs, problems with, 70–71
laser rot, 71
Lemcoe, M. M., 63, 69, 70
Lewis, George, 3
Library of Congress, 69; development of mass deacidification process, 52
Ligeti, Gyorgy, 27–28
Liszt, Franz, 18

magnetic media, bibliography, 77–80
Mannes College of Music, 20
MARC field 583, used for recording preservation treatment information, 54
markings, as variable in survey, 43, 44–45, 46
mass deacidification, background of, 51–52; costs, 56–57; at Northwestern University, 51–58; quality control in, 55–56
microfilming, 19–20
microforms, paper reproductions from, 8–9, 20, 22
moving image materials, preservation of, 59–74
music, notation, 8; preservation problems unique to, 5–11
music conservatory libraries, 12–34
Music Library Association, 1, 11, 30; *Newsletter,* 11; preservation activities, 10–11

music scores, 9–10; binding, 26–27; condition of, at Juilliard School, 35–50; dates on, 37; formats, 27–28; mass deacidification decisions, 52–53; paper used in, 29, 30
Music Publishers Association, 11, 30

National Archives, 68–69
National Bureau of Standards, 68–69
National Historical Publications and Records Commission, 17
New York Public Library, 8–9; Music Division, 20; Rodgers & Hammerstein Archives of Recorded Sound, 84–85
New York State Discretionary Grant Program for the Conservation and Preservation of Library Research Materials, 16–17
New York University, 20
Northeast Document Conservation Center, 15
Northwestern University, 2; Music Library, 51–58
Notes, 11

optical reflective surfaces, corrosion of, 63–64

pages, number of, as variable in survey, 40–41
paper, acid-free, use of for scores, 30; brittle, and country of origin, 45, 47, 38; brittle, and circulation, 46–47, 49; torn, as variable in survey, 43, 44; yellowing of, as variable in survey, 43, 44
Peabody Conservatory of Music, 33

pellon, 66–67
photocopying, for preservation of scores, 18, 19–20
Pickett, A. G., 63, 69, 70
preservation decision-making, 29–34
preservation programs, funding of, 15–17; in New York State, 15–17
preservation treatment information, recorded in MARC field 583, 54
Public Library Association, 1

recorded sound, *see* sound recordings
relative humidity, in preservation, 25
repair, as variable in survey, 45, 46
Rochester Institute of Technology, 64
Roosa, Mark, 1, 2–4

Sadewhite, Elizabeth, 2, 29, 30, 35–50
Scriabin, 8–9
Shackelton, Cheryl, 1
Shepard, John, 1
signatures, as variable in survey, 41
Society of American Archivists, 33
Sommer, Susan T., 5–11
sound recordings, 5–7; bibliography, 75–76; cleaning, 65–68; containers for, 68–69; at Juilliard School, 32–33; labels on, 65; materials used for, 61–62; preservation of, 59–74; preservation supplies, 81–83; reformatting, 84–89; storage environment, 69–72
Stanford University, Green Library, book condition survey, 35–36
Stockhausen, Karlheinz, 27, 28
Syracuse University, Belfer Audio Laboratory and Archive, 86–87

temperature, in preservation, 25
Townsend, John, 15

University of Texas, Historical Recordings Collection, 88–89

video recordings, at Juilliard School, 33–34
vinegar syndrome, 64

Xerox Corporation, 21

Yale University, 29; book condition survey, 36
Young, John Russell, 3

ML 111 .K65 1994

KNOWING THE SCORE